Hot Recipes in Cool Dishes™

— by Tara

Tara McConnell

Published by RR Donnelley

First paperback edition 2010

10 9 8 7 6 5 4 3

Author: Tara McConnell

Book design, food photographs and illustrations: by Christian and Elise Stella

Manufactured in the USA

ISBN 978-0-9841887-3-4

This book is dedicated to my father, my hero and biggest fan. My father is a constant source of inspiration and someone I aspire to be like every day.

Contents

INTRODUCTION

I can only assume that most people learn how to cook through trial and error, taking a cooking class, or even following along with a cooking show on television. Though I've gone through long trials and many errors in the kitchen, and though I've been known to watch a good amount of food television; I simply cannot give away any of the credit. Learning to bake, to broil, to sauté, and boil—learning how to cook—it all started with my mother.

Growing up, my mother and I spent a lot of our time in the kitchen. She would be cooking and I would be lying in the middle of the floor making fake snow angels and rambling on and on about my day. My mother never complained as she stepped over me to get around the kitchen, as this was our mother-daughter alone time. Instead, she would just tell me, step by step, what she was making and how she was making it. This is how I learned how to cook, this is where my love affair with the kitchen first began— lying in the middle of the floor.

When I was younger, my family always gathered for dinner. No matter what our day had brought us, when we sat down to dinner it was our time to reconnect with each other. Our time to share each and every nuance of our day.

I think, secretly, this was my mother's favorite time, not only to catch up with all of us, but to show her skills. My mother has always taken so much pride in preparing a family meal. Today I can realize that her use of food to express her love inspired me to share my gifts as well.

My sister and I always took on a job in the kitchen— she would set the table, I would clear the table, I would wash the dishes, she would dry them—with my mother cooking, we were happy to be responsible for everything else. Still, I always joked that my mother must have used every dish in the house to prepare her family meals. The sink overflowing and the counters scattered with pots, pans, baking dishes, serving bowls, plates, knives, and forks—I can only imagine that all of the time I spent washing dishes, subconsciously helped me to create temp-tations®.

Mom, Dad, and my sister Tracy

My temp-tations® presentable ovenware is unique, in that it makes one dish cooking truly one dish cooking—from prepping and mixing right in the dish, to serving, and eventually storing. As more and more people like you continue to embrace temp-tations®, I continue to see new and exciting ideas come to fruition. I continue to expand my collection with more choices in a greater variety.

But through it all, my number one request from people all over the country has been the very book you hold in your hands. A cookbook specifically written to fill your unique and beautiful temp-tations® dishes.

In this book are some of the very same recipes I ate growing up, the recipes that have been handed down from generation to generation—some written before temp-tations®

had ever been envisioned have been completely rewritten and tested to ensure that they utilize all of the advantages of temp-tations® presentable ovenware. There are also plenty of my newer, everyday favorites that I've been making in temp-tations® since I first came up with the recipe. I absolutely love all of the recipes in this book and feel that, between these pages, there is definitely something for everyone!

I hope this book inspires you to try some new dishes that can one day become your family favorites. Think of your meals as a blank canvas. Use my recipes, but feel free to add your own special twists. Make them YOUR recipes, so that they can become your "expressions of love" as my mother's cooking has always been for my family.

Hopefully, these recipes will not only add warmth to your meals, but also your hearts as you create memorable experiences with friends and family.

Pantry List

This is a list of everyday ingredients that would be good to have on hand when using this book. These are the items that pop up the most in my recipes with a good enough shelf life to purchase in advance. With these items in your cupboard and fridge, shopping for these recipes should be a breeze!

salt	grated Parmesan cheese
pepper	ketchup
garlic powder	mayonnaise
onion powder	all purpose flour
bay leaves	sugar
oregano	light brown sugar
basil	dark brown sugar
poultry seasoning	honey
Italian seasoning	jarred marinara sauce
paprika	jarred minced garlic
chili powder	butter or margarine
curry powder	eggs
ground ginger	milk
ground cinnamon	light cream (regular whipping cream)
nutmeg	baking soda
vanilla extract	baking powder
nonstick cooking spray	cornstarch
olive oil	chocolate chips
vegetable oil	yellow onions
balsamic vinegar	gold potatoes
cider vinegar	lemons

temp-tations® presentable ovenware is a way to cook your favorite meals (and soon-to-be new favorite meals within this book) effortlessly. With temp-tations®, the dish you cook in, is the dish you serve and store in. Each dish nestles in its matching basket that makes it truly oven to table. Classic styles from around the world in beautifully sculpted dishes are designed to complement any table and look so good that they never need to be hidden away in cabinets.

temp-tations® presentable ovenware is made of high quality and durable ceramic, which is…

-naturally nonstick

-oven safe up to 500 degrees

-dishwasher, microwave, refrigerator, and freezer safe

Each piece of temp-tations® **presentable ovenware** is unique, making them truly an art form. temp-tations® ceramicware is handcrafted and hand painted, therefore no two pieces are ever alike. Each set is truly one of a kind.

With a wide variety of colors, patterns, and sizes, I believe that temp-tations® has something for every kitchen, every dining room, and most important of all… everyone. It is our ambition to help you complete your set by designing new pieces for any and all of your kitchen and dining needs. With this book, I hope to have soon helped you complete a few delicious meals as well!

Each recipe in this book has been specifically written for and tested in temp-tations® **presentable ovenware**. Using temp-tations® **presentable ovenware** and this book, your meals should come out looking exactly as they do in the accompanying photographs. Each photograph was taken with un-altered food, prepared exactly to the specifications in the recipe.

As the designer, it is my goal to bring artistic beauty to everyone's dining experience.

Thank you for welcoming me into your home.

Tara

Appetizers

shown in temp-tations® Old World 2.5 quart rectangular baker

temp-tations®
presentable ovenware
by Tara

appetizers

Sweet and Sour Meatballs

This is my take on the tangy and classic party dish. With a sticky, sweet, and delicious sauce, you'll want to make sure you keep plenty of napkins handy! Though typically an appetizer, you could also serve these as an entrée over fluffy steamed rice and with a side of sautéed snow peas.

1. Preheat oven to 400 degrees. Place the sliced white bread in a dish of cold water for 5 minutes to moisten.

2. Remove the white bread from the dish and squeeze bread to drain water. Crumble the moistened bread into tiny pieces and place in a large mixing bowl. Cover with the ground beef, eggs, soy sauce, green onions, ground ginger, salt, and pepper.

3. Using your hands, combine all ingredients in mixing bowl and form into walnut-sized balls, arranging them in a single layer along the bottom of a large rectangular (4 or 5 quart) temp-tations® baking dish. Bake 30 minutes or until the meatballs are firm.

4. While the meatballs are cooking, drain the juice of the canned pineapple chunks into a sauce pot over medium-high heat. Add the apple cider vinegar, brown sugar, and ketchup to the pot and bring up to a boil, stirring constantly. Reduce heat to medium-low and simmer. Mix the cornstarch with 1-2 tablespoons of tap water and add to the sauce, simmering until thickened.

Shopping List

4 slices **white sandwich bread**

2 pounds **lean ground beef**

2 **large eggs**

2 tablespoons **reduced sodium soy sauce**

4 **green onions**, sliced

1 teaspoon **ground ginger**

½ teaspoon **salt**

¼ teaspoon **black pepper**

1 (**20** ounce) can **pineapple chunks**

¼ cup **apple cider vinegar**

¼ cup **dark brown sugar**

½ cup **ketchup**

2 teaspoons **cornstarch**

1 **red bell pepper**, cut into thin strips

5. Use tongs to transfer cooked meatballs to a 2.5 quart temp-tations® baking dish. Pour the sauce over the meatballs, add the canned pineapple chunks and red bell pepper strips, and stir all to combine. Bake an additional 10 minutes or until the sauce is bubbling hot. Garnish with additional sliced green onion, if you desire.

tips by Tara

Ground turkey or pork can be substituted in place of the ground beef. You can also use a bag of frozen meatballs by following their package directions and then starting this recipe at step 4.

| shown in temp-tations® 4 quart Cucina bowl

temp-tations
presentable ovenware
by Tara

Greek Pasta Salad

Pasta salads always make the best potluck dishes, as they don't require reheating once you arrive at your destination and only get better the longer that they sit! I like this Greek version with crumbled feta cheese as it offers a little something different than the usual Italian salads.

1. Boil rotini pasta according to the package directions, and then drain and rinse under cold water.

2. Place drained pasta in a 4 quart temp-tations® bowl or dish and cover with remaining ingredients.

3. Toss all ingredients until well combined, cover, and refrigerate for at least 2 hours to marinate before serving, although 4-6 hours is best. Stir well and serve sprinkled with additional oregano or a sprig of fresh oregano for garnish.

Shopping List

16 ounces **tri-color rotini**

1 jar (**12** ounces) quartered **artichoke hearts**, drained and rinsed

1 can (**6** ounces) **black olives**, drained

1 pint **cherry tomatoes**, halved

4 ounces crumbled **feta cheese**

1 bottle (**14-16** ounces) **Greek salad dressing**

¼ teaspoon **garlic powder**

¼ teaspoon **black pepper**

½ teaspoon **oregano**

tips by Tara

Any Italian salad dressing can be used in place of the Greek dressing, and shaved Parmesan cheese can be used in place of the feta cheese if you would prefer a more Italian salad.

appetizers

Sausage and Herbed Cheese Stuffed Mushrooms

These are excellent and disappear every time I make them. (Now I make two batches!) Everyone I've prepared this for raves and wants the recipe! The secret is using herbed cream cheese spread (cheapest is usually Philadelphia brand) in place of ordinary cream cheese to add a ton of flavors in just that one ingredient.

1. Preheat oven to 375 degrees. Snap stems from mushroom caps, and finely chop stems by hand or with a quick pulse in a food processor.

2. In a skillet over medium-high heat, brown sausage, about 5 minutes, crumbling with a spatula as you brown. Add chopped stems and cook an additional 3 minutes. Remove from heat and drain any excess liquid.

3. Add cream cheese, spinach, oregano, salt, and pepper to the sausage mixture and mix well to finish the filling.

4. Toss mushroom caps in 1 tablespoon of the olive oil and arrange cup-side up in a 4 quart temp-tations® baking dish. Spoon a portion of the filling into each cap.

5. Combine breadcrumbs with the remaining olive oil and top each mushroom with a pinch. Bake 30 minutes, or until topping is browned and crispy. Serve hot.

Shopping List

1 ½ pounds medium **button mushrooms**

½ pound **mild Italian sausage**, removed from casing

6 ounces **herbed cream cheese spread**

1 cup **frozen chopped spinach**, defrosted and water squeezed out

1 teaspoon **dried oregano**

½ teaspoon **salt**

¼ teaspoon **black pepper**

2 tablespoons **olive oil**

½ cup **Italian seasoned breadcrumbs**

tips by Tara

For more traditional sausage stuffed mushrooms, simply skip the spinach and oregano, substitute pork breakfast sausage in place of the Italian, and go with regular cream cheese in place of the herbed spread.

Prep Time	Cook Time		Serves	1
10 mins	**0** mins		**8**	**Quart**

temp-tations®
presentable ovenware
by Tara

Mom's Guacamole

My mother always makes fresh guacamole for parties, as it is a relatively inexpensive, yet hearty, appetizer that is always appreciated more than just chips and dip! Not only does fresh lime juice perfectly complement the avocado, it also keeps the avocado from turning brown, so remember to get the lime juice onto the avocadoes immediately after scooping them into the bowl.

1. Slice avocadoes in half, rotating around the pit with your knife. Scoop out pits and discard.

2. Using a large spoon, scoop all avocadoes from their skin and place in a 1 quart temp-tations® mixing bowl.

Shopping List

3 Hass avocadoes
2 cloves **garlic**, smashed or minced
¼ cup **chunky salsa**
¼ cup **sour cream**
juice of **1** small **lime**
salt to taste

3. Cover avocadoes in bowl with remaining ingredients, and then use a heavy spoon (an ice cream scooper works well) to mash everything together, forming a thick and chunky dip.

4. Serve right in the temp-tations® mixing bowl, garnished with fresh cilantro, if desired. Serve alongside tortilla chips.

tips by Tara

If you like a smoother guacamole, you can puree the avocado in a food processor before transferring to the mixing bowl. You can also serve this guacamole in my temp-tations® Old World 3 piece chip and dip server. Use the tray's three compartments to serve alongside tortilla chips, pita chips, and fresh veggies!

Prep Time	Cook Time		Serves	**4**
1.5 hours	**22** mins		**8**	**Quart**

temp-tations®
presentable ovenware
by Tara

appetizers

Focaccia Bread

Focaccia Bread is a chewy, pizza-like bread, topped with olive oil and Italian spices. I like it best with thin slices of onion, colorful bell peppers, and fresh tomato. The key is slicing the vegetables so thin that they literally bake right onto the top of the bread. You can also use this recipe as a homemade pizza dough simply by following through step 4.

1. In a small bowl, combine yeast with 1 ¼ cups warm tap water and let sit for 15 minutes to activate yeast. (Set your faucet almost all the way to hot.)

2. In a large mixing bowl, combine flour, sugar, and salt. Pour activated water and yeast mixture into the dry ingredients, and then add 1 tablespoon of the olive oil. Mix all until a sticky dough is formed.

3. Transfer to a well floured surface and knead, adding additional flour, just until no longer sticky. Return ball of dough to the mixing bowl, cover with a damp cloth, and set in a warm place to rise for 1 hour.

4. On a well floured surface, use a rolling pin to roll out dough, until it is a large ⅓ inch thick rectangle. Spray a 4 quart temp-tations® baking dish with nonstick cooking spray and then transfer the large rectangle of dough into the dish. Pull the dough towards the walls of the dish to mostly cover the bottom of the dish.

5. Preheat the oven to 400 degrees. Drizzle the entire surface of the dough with the remaining 2 tablespoons of olive oil. Sprinkle garlic powder, Italian seasoning, and Parmesan cheese over top. Top sporadically with extremely thin slices of red onion, bell peppers, tomato, or any combination of the three. Bake 20-22 minutes, or until golden brown.

Shopping List

1 packet (¼ ounce) **active dry yeast**

3 ¼ cups **all purpose flour**

1 ½ teaspoons **sugar**

1 teaspoon **salt**

3 tablespoons **olive oil**

nonstick cooking spray

½ teaspoon **garlic powder**

¾ teaspoon **Italian seasoning**

2 tablespoons grated **Parmesan cheese**

thinly sliced **red onion, bell peppers,** or **tomatoes**

tips by Tara

For a warm place to rise the dough, set your oven to its lowest setting for 2-3 minutes, turn off, and then place dough in oven with oven door open.

appetizers

Jalapeño Hummus

I love hummus, a creamy, thick dip made from garbanzo beans—but one of the main ingredients in a classic hummus is a hard to find sesame seed paste called tahini. In my recipe, I use the spicy, southwestern flavors of diced jalapeños and salsa in place of the tahini for something entirely new and incredibly addictive! Made in only minutes, this recipe is great way to show off some of your smaller pieces of temp-tations®, as a little hummus goes a long way.

Shopping List

1. Drain and rinse garbanzo beans.

1 can (14-16 ounces) **garbanzo beans (chickpeas)**

¼ cup **canned jalapeños**, drained

juice of **1** small **lemon**

2. Place all ingredients in the bowl of a food processor and pulse until smooth and creamy, about 2 minutes.

2 tablespoons **chunky salsa**

2 teaspoons **minced garlic**

salt to taste

3. Salt to taste and serve in a 1 quart temp-tations® mixing bowl or baking dish. Refrigerating at least 2 hours will bring the flavor out even more. Serve alongside pita chips or thick tortilla chips.

tips by Tara

For a milder dip, use ¼ cup canned diced green chiles in place of the jalapeños. If the dip is too thick for your liking, simply thin it out with a few teaspoons of olive oil.

Prep Time
10 mins

Cook Time
20 mins

Serves
12

1.5 Quart

temp-tations
presentable ovenware
by Tara

appetizers

Queso Fundido

This Mexican cheese dip is great for game days or parties. Buy mild, medium, or hot salsa to use, whichever you prefer, but be warned that the chili powder does add a bit of a kick as well! This makes a whole lot of queso, so be sure to buy a large bag of tortilla chips!

1. Preheat oven to 350 degrees.

2. In a 1.5 quart temp-tations® baking dish, combine cream cheese and sour cream, mixing until smooth.

3. Stir in chili powder, salsa, and oregano. Top with the shredded cheese and bake 15-20 minutes, or until cheese is melted and mixture is bubbly. Serve hot, with tortilla chips for dipping. Garnish with fresh diced tomato and fresh cilantro, if desired.

Shopping List

8 ounces **cream cheese**, regular or reduced fat, softened

16 ounces **sour cream**, regular or reduced fat

1 tablespoon **chili powder**

1 cup **chunky salsa**

1 teaspoon **dried oregano**

2 cups shredded **Monterey jack cheese**

tips by Tara

If your crowd likes it spicy, add ¼ pound of diced and browned chorizo and substitute pepper jack cheese for Monterey jack. You can also try spreading the finished queso into warm flour tortillas, topping with sautéed onions, bell peppers, and grilled chicken, and then rolling up for a cheesy fajita.

| shown in temp-tations® Toile 1 quart baker, with chips in 2.5 quart baker

Prep Time	Cook Time		Serves	1
15 mins	**25** mins		**8**	**Quart**

temp-tations
presentable ovenware
by Tara

appetizers

Spinach and Artichoke Dip

I love making hot dips in my 1 quart bakers. They're just the right size for a small get together with friends. Of course, if you have more than a few friends over, the recipe is easily doubled for one of my 2 quart bakers!

1. Preheat oven to 400 degrees.

2. Mix all ingredients until well combined and spread into a 1 quart temp-tations® baking dish. Microwaving cream cheese for 30-45 seconds to soften will make the mixing far easier. You can also mix directly in the baking dish, but you will have to add the spinach in a little at a time as it will be bulkier than the dish until submerged.

3. Bake for 20-25 minutes or until dip is bubbling and top is lightly browned. Serve with tortilla chips, root chips, toasted baguette slices, or hearty crackers.

Shopping List

1 cup **artichoke hearts**, drained and roughly chopped

½ cup grated **Parmesan cheese**

1 cup **sour cream**, regular or reduced fat

4 ounces **cream cheese**, regular or reduced fat

1 ½ cups fresh **spinach**, roughly chopped

2 teaspoons **minced garlic**

¼ teaspoon **salt**

⅛ teaspoon **pepper**

tips by Tara

This is best when it is nice and hot, so if it cools down before it is all gone, simply microwave for 1 minute, until bubbly hot once again.

Jenn's East Meets West Chicken Wings

These wings, by my childhood friend, Jenn, are messy to make and messy to eat, so have plenty of napkins ready while you watch them disappear! These wings look as delicious as they taste, with a rich browned skin straight out of the oven. The mysterious Asian flavor comes from Chinese five-spice powder. If you don't have it on hand, it's easy to make your own by reading my tip below.

1. In a large mixing bowl, combine soy sauce, molasses, honey, chili sauce, garlic, and Chinese five-spice to make a marinade. Transfer ½ of the marinade to a separate container and reserve for topping the wings in step 5.

2. Add wings to the mixing bowl and toss to coat in marinade. Cover and refrigerate for at least 2 hours (overnight is best), tossing halfway through to evenly marinate.

Shopping List

½ cup **reduced sodium soy sauce**

½ cup **molasses**

¼ cup **honey**

¼ cup **chili sauce**

1 tablespoon **minced garlic**

1 ½ teaspoons **Chinese five-spice powder**

3 pounds **chicken wings**, thawed if frozen

6 **green onions**, sliced

3. Preheat oven to 400 degrees. Remove chicken wings from marinade and transfer to a 3.5 quart temp-tations® baking dish. Discard used marinade.

4. Bake about 45 minutes, turning halfway through, until the wings are cooked throughout, well browned, and crispy.

5. Drizzle cooked wings with the reserved marinade from step 1 and sprinkle with green onions before serving.

tips by Tara

To make your own seasoning similar to Chinese five-spice powder, combine ½ teaspoon each of cinnamon, black pepper, and allspice.

Prep Time	Cook Time		Serves	1.5
15 mins	**0** mins		**16**	**Quart**

temp-tations
presentable ovenware
by Tara

appetizers

Green Olive and Artichoke Spread

Olives and artichokes grow all along the shores of the Mediterranean, and this spread is a lot like a French tapenade, usually made with olives and other good things, like the artichokes used here. I make my version with cream cheese to give it a nice, spreadable consistency for serving alongside crackers or toasted bread rounds.

1. Place the cream cheese in the bowl of a food processor and pulse until creamy and soft, about 1 minute.

2. Transfer cream cheese to a 1.5 quart temp-tations® baking dish (There is no need to clean out food processor before proceeding).

3. Place the remaining ingredients in the bowl of the food processor and pulse until very finely chopped but not pureed, about 1 minute.

Shopping List

2 (**8 ounces**) packages **light cream cheese,** softened

2 cups **pimento-stuffed green olives,** drained

1 (**12 ounce**) jar **marinated artichoke hearts,** drained

½ cup **parsley leaves**

zest and juice of **1 lemon**

2 teaspoons **minced garlic**

1 teaspoon **dried thyme**

¼ teaspoon **black pepper**

4. Combine the olive mixture with the cream cheese, mixing well. Serve chilled or at room temperature, garnished with lemon slices and a sprig of parsley, if desired.

tips by Tara

To lower the sodium content of this spread, rinse the olives extremely well to wash away some of their salty brine. Black olives or pitted kalamata olives can also be used in place of the green. Or try a mixture of all three olives!

shown in temp-tations® Old World Embossed 5 quart rectangular baker

Prep Time | Cook Time | Serves
20 mins | **15** mins | 6 | **5** Quart

temp-tations
presentable ovenware
by Tara

appetizers

Buffalo Chicken Pizza Bagels

With these fantastically easy pizza bagels, you'll get all of the flavor you would with Buffalo style wings, just without all the mess. Whether it's a casual night at home with family or a Sunday sports event with your neighborhood pals, these are sure to score some big points!

1. Preheat oven to 400 degrees. Place mini bagel halves, crust side down, in a single layer along the bottom of a 5 quart temp-tations® baking dish.

2. In a large skillet over medium-high heat, sauté 1 tablespoon of the butter and onions until onions begin to caramelize, about 7 minutes.

3. Add chicken, hot sauce, and remaining butter to the skillet and stir all to combine.

Shopping List

6 mini bagels, split

3 tablespoons **butter** or **margarine**

1 small **yellow onion**, thinly sliced

8 ounces **cooked chicken**, diced

1 tablespoon **Louisiana hot sauce** (**2** for spicy)

½ cup crumbled **bleu cheese**

½ cup shredded **mozzarella cheese**

4. Top each bagel half with an equal amount of the chicken and onion mixture from the skillet. Sprinkle crumbled bleu cheese over all, and then top with mozzarella cheese.

5. Bake 12-15 minutes, or until bagel bottoms are browned and crispy, and cheese is melted. Serve hot.

tips by Tara

You can also skip topping the bagels with crumbled bleu cheese and simply serve them alongside a chunky bleu cheese dressing for dipping.

Prep Time
15 mins

Cook Time
10 mins

Serves
10

4
Quart

temp-tations
presentable ovenware
by Tara

Balsamic Bruschetta

This is a quick and easy recipe that never fails to please! Balsamic vinegar adds a beautiful dark color and sweet taste to the tomato based spread served alongside toasted Italian bread in this very simple, yet elegant, appetizer.

1. Preheat oven to 400 degrees. Arrange bread in a single layer at the bottom of a 4 quart temp-tations® baking dish.

2. Bake bread 10 minutes or until lightly browned.

3. In a temp-tations® mixing bowl, combine tomatoes, pesto, Parmesan cheese, oil, vinegar, salt, and pepper. Toss gently and let marinate for 20 minutes at room temperature.

4. Just before serving, spoon 1 tablespoon of the tomato spread onto each slice of toast, arranging on a temp-tations® serving platter or serving directly in the 4 quart baking dish. You can also serve the tomato spread alongside the toasted bread for guests to serve themselves.

Shopping List

1 loaf sliced **Italian bread**, each slice cut in half

2 cups diced **fresh tomatoes**

¼ cup jarred **pesto sauce**

¼ cup shredded or grated **Parmesan cheese**

2 tablespoons **olive oil**

2 tablespoons **balsamic vinegar**

½ teaspoon **salt**

¼ teaspoon **black pepper**

tips by Tara

This dip tastes best at room temperature, so if there is any left, bring it out of the refrigerator for an hour before serving. If fresh tomatoes are not in season, simply substitute 2 well drained cans of petite diced tomatoes. A sliced French baguette can be substituted for the Italian bread, with no need to slice the slices in half again. A few chopped leaves of fresh basil can be substituted for the jarred pesto sauce.

appetizers

Prep Time
30 mins

Cook Time
0 mins

Serves
8

2 Quart

temp-tations
presentable ovenware
by Tara

Cucumber and Peanut Salad

This refreshing cucumber salad is both sweet and sour and packs a nice crunch! Though cucumber salads are usually made with Mediterranean flavors, I've made this one with the Asian flavors of rice wine vinegar and ground ginger. To make a more American cucumber salad, see my tips below.

1. In a 2 quart or larger temp-tations® bowl or baking dish, combine vinegar, oil, sugar, ginger, salt, and pepper.

2. Add cucumbers and red onion, and marinate 15 minutes, either in the refrigerator or at room temperature.

3. Drain through a colander and return to the temp-tations® bowl or dish.

Shopping List

½ cup **rice wine vinegar**

⅓ cup **vegetable oil**

2 tablespoons **sugar**

1 teaspoon **ground ginger**

1 teaspoon **salt**

¼ teaspoon **black pepper**

3 medium **cucumbers**, peeled and sliced

¼ cup chopped **red onion**

½ cup **chopped roasted peanuts**

4. Add peanuts to marinated cucumber, toss all to combine, and serve.

tips by Tara

Rice wine vinegar can be found in either the ordinary vinegar section or the Asian foods aisle of the grocery store, though 6 tablespoons of apple cider vinegar can also be used in its place. Make a more American salad by using the apple cider vinegar, skipping the ground ginger, and substituting sliced almonds in place of the peanuts.

Prep Time Cook Time Serves 2.5
10 mins 10 mins 8 Quart
temp-tations
presentable ovenware
by Tara

appetizers

Loaded Potato Chips

These chips have all of the great flavors of potato skins, only they are amazingly easier to make! The perfect party or game day appetizer, sometimes the simplest things are the most satisfying.

1. Preheat oven to 350 degrees.

2. Place ½ of the potato chips into a 2.5 quart temp-tations® baking dish, and cover with ½ of the shredded sharp Cheddar cheese and ½ of the bacon pieces.

3. Add the remaining chips, and cover with the remaining Cheddar and bacon. Bake for 8-10 minutes, until cheese is melted and bubbly.

4. Top with a large dollop of sour cream (or serve on the side for dipping), and sprinkle with sliced green onions before serving hot.

Shopping List

1 bag (**9-12** ounces) **kettle cooked potato chips**

1 rounded cup shredded **sharp Cheddar cheese**

⅓ cup crumbled **bacon pieces**

1 cup **sour cream**, regular or reduced fat

2 green onions, sliced

tips by Tara

You can find already cooked and crumbled real bacon pieces in the salad dressing aisle, which really makes this recipe a snap!

Prep Time

30
mins

Cook Time

1
hour

Serves

10

4
Quart

temp-tations
presentable ovenware
by Tara

Roasted Eggplant and Feta Spread

This Mediterranean eggplant spread is an unusual mix of ingredients that blend together in the most delicious way! A great dish for entertaining because you can make it up to two days ahead and serve chilled (though it's also good warmed through in the microwave) with pita chips, warm pita bread, sliced vegetables, or crackers.

1. Preheat oven to 400 degrees. Arrange the eggplant quarters in a 4-quart temp-tations® baking dish and cover with aluminum foil. Bake until the eggplant is soft, about 1 hour.

2. Place olive oil in a small skillet over medium to medium-high heat and lightly brown the walnuts and garlic, about 3 minutes. Remove from heat and let cool until preparing the spread.

3. Refrigerate eggplant 30 minutes, or until cooled. Use a pointed spoon to scoop out the soft eggplant meat, discarding skin. Transfer meat to a colander to drain excess liquid, about 5 minutes.

4. Place eggplant meat, cooked walnut mixture, and all remaining ingredients in the bowl of a food processor and pulse until the mixture is chunky but holds together. Transfer to a 2.5 quart or larger temp-tations® bowl or dish to serve.

Shopping List

3 medium **eggplants**, quartered

2 tablespoons **olive oil**

1 ½ cups **walnuts**

1 tablespoon **minced garlic**

2 cups crumbled **feta cheese**

2 tablespoons **red wine vinegar**

2 tablespoons chopped **dill**, or **2** teaspoons **dried dill**

¼ teaspoon **black pepper**

tips by *Tara*

I would definitely recommend this, even if you are not the biggest fan of eggplant. This can also be used as a sandwich spread or even warm over pasta.

appetizers

Prep Time

Cook Time

Serves

10
mins

0
mins

12

1
Quart

temp-tations
presentable ovenware
by Tara

appetizers

Peanut Butter Fruit and Snack Dip

This is definitely a party dip that you don't see every day, yet it is a surprisingly versatile dish. It pairs well with just about anything you can dip, other than chips. Serve it with sliced apples, crackers (especially cheese crackers!), pretzels, and anything that goes well with peanut butter! Using 2 cups of low fat vanilla yogurt with 1 cup of peanut butter helps "stretch" the peanut butter taste, while making the final dip include only ⅓ the fat of peanut butter alone!

1. Place all ingredients in a 1 quart temp-tations® mixing bowl or baking dish.

2. Fold all ingredients together until smooth and creamy. (Combining with a food processor is easier on your arm, but not necessary.)

Shopping List

1 cup **creamy peanut butter**, room temperature

2 cups **low fat vanilla yogurt**

1 tablespoon **honey**

chopped peanuts, optional, for garnish

3. Top with a handful of chopped peanuts, for garnish. Serve alongside apple slices and other fruit, apple chips, cheese crackers, pretzels, or graham crackers for dipping. You can also use as a lighter sandwich spread in place of regular peanut butter.

tips by Tara

Try folding in a handful of raisins and serving alongside celery sticks for a sort of deconstructed version of "Ants on a Log". Or try using a spoon to make a small indention in the middle of the finished dip, and using an ice cream scooper to fill it with a scoop of your favorite jam or preserves for a Peanut Butter and Jelly Dip.

shown transferred to a temp-tations® Old World serving platter

temp-tations®
presentable ovenware
by Tara

Asparagus Swizzle Sticks

This fancy appetizer is surprisingly simple to make, and a really unique way to set your parties or holiday gatherings apart. The title of this recipe comes from my favorite way of serving—alongside hot soup for swirling and dipping.

1. Preheat oven to 400 degrees. Spray a large rectangular temp-tations® baking dish with nonstick cooking spray; the larger, the better. Or bake right on one of my temp-tations® serving platters.

2. Trim 1 ½ to 2 inches off the bottom of the stalks of asparagus and discard.

3. Place asparagus spears in a large food storage bag and add the olive oil, garlic powder, salt, and pepper. Shake all to evenly coat.

4. Unroll pizza crust and slice into long strips about ¼ inch wide.

Shopping List

nonstick cooking spray

1 pound asparagus spears

1 tablespoon **olive oil**

¼ teaspoon **garlic powder**

¼ teaspoon **salt**

⅛ teaspoon **pepper**

1 can (**11** ounces) **thin pizza crust** (such as Pillsbury)

2 tablespoons grated **Parmesan cheese**

5. Spin 1 strip of the dough around the asparagus like the striping of a barber's pole, and then place wrapped asparagus in the greased baking dish.

6. Once baking dish is full, sprinkle all wrapped asparagus with Parmesan cheese and bake for 10-12 minutes, or until puffy and golden brown. Serve immediately. Note: I usually have enough dough and asparagus to make 2 full batches of 16 pieces each.

tips by Tara

When buying the asparagus, look for asparagus that are about as thick as a pencil. Asparagus that are too thick may not cook all the way through before the dough is browned.

appetizers

Prep Time
10
mins

Cook Time
6
mins

Serves
10

1.5
Quart

temp-tations
presentable ovenware
by Tara

Cheesy Refried Bean Dip

Though I know that everyone has a version of a processed cheese (like Velveeta) dip, I decided to share mine, which is thick with refried beans and full of flavor thanks to four added spices. Serve alongside tortilla chips, or even inside flour tortillas with rice to make quick and easy burritos.

1. Place refried beans, chunky salsa, garlic powder, onion powder, chili powder, and cumin in a 1.5 quart temp-tations® baking dish, and stir to combine.

2. Top with processed cheese, cover with plastic wrap, and pierce the center of the plastic wrap with a fork to vent air. Microwave on high for 3 minutes.

Shopping List

1 can (**16** ounces) **refried beans**

1 cup **chunky salsa**

¼ teaspoon **garlic powder**

¼ teaspoon **onion powder**

¼ teaspoon **chili powder**

¼ teaspoon **cumin**

1 rounded cup cubed **processed cheese** (like Velveeta)

3. Peel back plastic wrap, stir well, and then re-cover and microwave on high for an additional 3 minutes, or until very hot and bubbly. Stir well and serve immediately.

tips by Tara

You can also use 8 slices of American cheese or one 8 ounce brick of cream cheese in place of the processed cheese. Reduced fat processed cheese or even fat free cream cheese works extremely well too.

Brunch

Prep Time	Cook Time		Serves	4
2 hours	**22** mins		**12**	**Quart**

temp-tations
presentable ovenware
by Tara

brunch

Cinnamon Rolls

While temp-tations® is also great for baking store bought, canned cinnamon rolls, you have to at least make them from scratch once in your life! There is nothing like a fresh, homemade cinnamon roll straight out of the oven, and though this recipe is not the easiest in this book, it's definitely one of the best!

1. In a large mixing bowl, whisk eggs until frothy. Whisk in yeast, milk, and melted butter and let sit for 10 minutes.

2. Add the remaining *Dough* ingredients and mix into a sticky dough. Transfer to a well floured surface and knead, adding additional flour, just until no longer sticky. Return ball of dough to the mixing bowl, cover, and place in a warm place to rise for 1 hour.

3. On a well floured surface, use a rolling pin to roll out dough, until it is a large ¼ inch thick rectangle. Spread the softened butter on the surface of the dough to start the filling. Combine brown sugar and cinnamon, and sprinkle evenly over the buttered dough.

4. Spray a 4 quart temp-tations® baking dish with nonstick cooking spray. Grab the short side of the dough and roll entire dough into a pinwheel, pressing firmly as you go. Slice rolled pinwheel into 1 ¼ inch thick rounds and place into baking dish. It's okay if they are touching. You should have enough rounds to fill the dish. Cover and let rise in a warm place for another 30 minutes.

5. Preheat oven to 400 degrees and bake cinnamon rolls 18-22 minutes, or until the tops are golden brown. Combine melted butter and powdered sugar to create the icing. If icing is hard, microwave 10-15 seconds to soften. Spoon icing over cinnamon rolls while still hot, and serve.

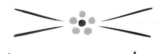

Shopping List

DOUGH

2 large **eggs**

1 packet (¼ ounce) **active dry yeast**

1 cup **milk**, heated until warm

5 tablespoons **butter** or **margarine**, melted

3 ½ cups **all purpose flour**

½ cup **Bisquick baking mix**

½ cup **sugar**

¾ teaspoon **salt**

FILLING

5 tablespoons **butter** or **margarine**, softened

1 cup **dark brown sugar**

1 tablespoon **ground cinnamon**

ICING

3 tablespoons **butter** or **margarine**, melted

1 cup **powdered sugar**

tips by Tara

For a warm place to let the dough rise, set your oven to its lowest setting for 2-3 minutes. Turn off, and then place dough in oven, with oven door open.

Prep Time Cook Time Serves 1

15 1 6 Quart
mins hour

temp-tations
presentable ovenware
by Tara

Quiche Lorraine

When I want something home-cooked and satisfying, I often reach for this recipe. This quiche definitely tastes as good cold as it does warm from the oven, especially when served alongside hot soup. With bacon, Swiss cheese, and onion, Quiche Lorraine is always the favorite amongst quiches.

1. Preheat oven to 425 degrees. Unroll pie crust and place in a 1 quart temp-tations® pie plate. Fold down and press top of crust into fluted edges of the pie plate.

2. In a mixing bowl, combine bacon, cheese, onion, and flour. Toss all to coat. Pour into pie crust in baking dish.

3. In a large mixing bowl, beat together eggs, cream, nutmeg, salt, and pepper. Pour over other ingredients in pie crust.

Shopping List

1 rolled **9 inch pie crust**, room temperature

12 slices **pre-cooked bacon**, chopped

2 cups shredded **Swiss cheese**

½ cup chopped **yellow onion**

2 tablespoons **all purpose flour**

4 eggs

2 cups **light cream**

¼ teaspoon **nutmeg**

½ teaspoon **salt**

¼ teaspoon **black pepper**

4. Bake for 15 minutes and then reduce oven's temperature to 300 degrees and bake 45 minutes longer, or until a toothpick inserted into the center comes out mostly clean. Let sit 10 minutes before slicing into 6 pieces.

tips by Tara

I like to add a cup of cooked vegetables, such as broccoli, mushrooms, or spinach to the quiche before baking. A small pinch of cayenne pepper will add a little spice.

brunch

Bananas Foster Oatmeal

I'm not exactly sure why so many people have switched to instant oatmeal when you can cook a breakfast like this from traditional oats and a real banana in less than 5 minutes, using only temp-tations® and your microwave! This recipe also makes a very hearty two portions.

1. Peel and dice banana and place in a 1.5 quart temp-tations® mixing bowl or baking dish.

2. Cover with remaining ingredients and stir to combine.

3. Microwave on high 4 ½ minutes, or until oatmeal is very bubbly. Carefully remove from microwave (dish will be very hot!) and stir well. Let cool at least 5 minutes before serving. Add any additional white sugar to taste.

Shopping List

1 ripe **banana**
1 ¼ cups **rolled oats** (non-instant oatmeal)
2 cups **milk**
1 tablespoon **butter** or **margarine**
2 tablespoons **dark brown sugar**
1 tablespoon **sugar**
¼ teaspoon **ground cinnamon**
¼ teaspoon **vanilla extract**
⅛ teaspoon **salt**

tips by Tara

Mash one half of the banana before adding to the oatmeal in step 1 for even more banana flavor throughout. You can also use this exact same recipe with one peeled, cored, and diced apple in place of the banana, though apples will not release as much of their flavor into the oatmeal.

shown in temp-tations® Old World Embossed 3 quart rectangular baker

Cheesy Ham and Broccoli "Spoonbread"

Real spoonbread is a soft, doughy, cornmeal casserole doled out by the spoon. My recipe substitutes a soft biscuit dough filled with mounds of ham, broccoli, and Cheddar cheese. The cheese and broccoli practically bake right into the dough for something entirely new and extremely delicious. While the idea of eating a soft, doughy, casserole with a spoon may not sound all that good now, you just have to trust me on this one!

1. Preheat oven to 350 degrees. Spray a 3.5 quart temp-tations® baking dish with nonstick cooking spray.

2. Place cubed ham, broccoli florets, and Cheddar cheese in the greased baking dish and toss lightly to combine.

3. In a mixing bowl, combine Bisquick, milk, and eggs, stirring until a thick batter is created. Pour batter over top all in baking dish and then spread evenly.

4. Drizzle the melted butter over top of the batter in the baking dish, and then sprinkle with the onion powder.

5. Bake for 55-60 minutes, or until top is golden brown and center feels mostly springy. Let cool 10 minutes before serving... with a spoon!

Shopping List

nonstick cooking spray

16 ounces **cubed ham**

14 ounces **frozen broccoli florets**, thawed and drained

2 cups **shredded Cheddar cheese**

3 cups **Bisquick baking mix**

1 ¾ cups **milk**

2 large **eggs**

2 tablespoons **butter** or **margarine**, melted

¼ teaspoon **onion powder**

tips by Tara

You can also make this with reduced fat Cheddar cheese and reduced fat Bisquick to lighten things up. You can also skip the melted butter on top to lighten it up further.

brunch

brunch

Waldorf Chicken Salad

This combination of two cold and creamy salads, one with chicken and one with apples, is one of my favorite ways to prepare chicken salad. I like to mix a couple of different kinds of apples, like sweet Golden Delicious and tart Granny Smith, and serve it on a bed of tender lettuce leaves.

1. In a 2 quart or larger temp-tations® mixing bowl or baking dish, combine mayonnaise, lemon juice, nutmeg, salt, and pepper.

2. Add the chicken, apples, walnuts, and celery, and gently fold all together.

3. Serve chilled, garnished with additional walnuts.

Shopping List

¾ cup **mayonnaise**, regular or reduced fat

Juice of **1 lemon**

¼ teaspoon **ground nutmeg**

½ teaspoon **salt**

¼ teaspoon **black pepper**

3 cups **cooked chicken**, shredded or diced

3 apples, cored and chopped

½ cup **chopped walnuts**

¾ cup chopped **celery**

tips by Tara

To make this salad even easier to prepare, buy a supermarket rotisserie chicken. If you like, you can toast the walnuts in a skillet over medium to medium-high heat for a few minutes to enhance their warm, nutty flavor. You can also peel the apples, but I prefer to leave on their vitamin-packed, colorful skins. Adding a handful of dried cranberries or topping with bleu cheese crumbles is also very good.

temp-tations
presentable ovenware
by Tara

Cheesy Hash Brown Casserole

Cheesy, creamy, and delicious, this delectable hash brown casserole has a crunchy cornflake topping that makes it irresistible. Enough to feed the whole crowd for Sunday brunch, and if a crowd isn't around, you'll be glad to have leftovers!

brunch

1. Preheat oven to 350 degrees.

2. In a 3.5 quart temp-tations® baking dish, combine potatoes, 2 tablespoons of the melted butter, cream of onion soup, sour cream, onion, green bell pepper, Cheddar cheese, and black pepper. Mix well and spread evenly throughout the dish.

3. Toss cornflakes in the remaining melted butter and sprinkle over top casserole.

Shopping List

1 (2 pound) package **frozen hash brown potatoes,** thawed

4 tablespoons **butter** or **margarine,** melted

1 (10 ounce) can **condensed cream of onion soup**

1 cup **reduced fat sour cream**

½ cup chopped **onion**

½ cup chopped **green bell pepper**

2 cups shredded **sharp Cheddar cheese**

¼ teaspoon **black pepper**

1 cup crushed **cornflakes cereal**

4. Bake 40 minutes or until browned and bubbling. Cool 10 minutes before serving.

tips by Tara

For a full breakfast, add 8 ounces diced ham or cooked crumbled breakfast sausage in step 2 and serve baked casserole topped with fried or scrambled eggs.

Prep Time
20 mins

Cook Time
50 mins

Serves
8

3.5
Quart

temp-tations
presentable ovenware
by Tara

Turkey Sausage Strata

Stratas are a lot like savory bread puddings, perfect for breakfast or brunch with a crowd, as you can serve 8 people from one dish prepared the night before. I like to use turkey sausage in place of pork sausage to make this hearty dish just a little bit lighter.

brunch

1. Spray a 3.5 quart temp-tations® baking dish with nonstick cooking spray.

2. Break Italian bread into 1 inch pieces and place in baking dish. Bread should fill the dish about half way.

3. In a large skillet over medium-high heat, cook turkey sausage until well browned. Crumble the sausage as it cooks, especially if using breakfast links. Remove from heat, and then drain any excess grease.

4. In a large bowl, whisk together eggs, milk, salt, and pepper. Pour over bread in baking dish.

Shopping List

nonstick cooking spray

1 small loaf **Italian bread**

12 ounces **turkey breakfast sausage**

5 eggs

1 ½ cups **milk**

¼ teaspoon **salt**

⅛ teaspoon **black pepper**

3 green onions, sliced

2 cups shredded **Cheddar cheese**

5. Add sliced green onions and cooked turkey sausage to the baking dish, stirring until all are combined. Top with Cheddar cheese, cover, and chill for at least 2 hours (overnight is best).

6. Preheat oven to 350 degrees, uncover, and bake strata for 45-50 minutes, or until cheese is well browned and the strata is set.

tips by Tara

Though it may not seem necessary, I highly recommend preparing this the night before, as the bread really softens as it chills, becoming a part of the strata, rather than just cubes of bread surrounded by egg.

Prep Time
20
mins

Cook Time
0
mins

Serves
4

3
Quart

temp-tations
presentable ovenware
by Tara

Everything Chopped Salad

Though I'll admit that I usually just throw a little of everything into my chopped salads, this combination with broccoli, Cheddar cheese, egg, bacon, and onion is one of my favorites, especially when paired with a creamy dressing.

1. Place chopped lettuce in my 12 inch fluted salad bowl, or any 3 quart temp-tations® dish.

2. Arrange remaining ingredients in neat rows for the best presentation. Serve alongside ranch, creamy Italian, or any creamy salad dressing.

3. At the table, I like to add about ⅔ cup of dressing to the bowl and toss all before serving.

Shopping List

1 small head **iceberg lettuce**, chopped

2 hard boiled eggs, chopped

1 large **tomato**, chopped

⅔ cup chopped **yellow onion**

½ cup crumbled **bacon pieces**

⅔ cup chopped **broccoli**

⅔ cup crumbled or cubed **Cheddar cheese**

your favorite **creamy salad dressing**

tips by Tara

You can make your own Creamy Italian Dressing by mixing ⅔ cup mayonnaise with 2 tablespoons red wine vinegar, 1 tablespoon finely minced red onion, 1 teaspoon sugar, 1 teaspoon Italian seasoning, ¼ teaspoon garlic powder, and salt and pepper to taste.

brunch

Prep Time

20 mins

Cook Time

20 mins

Serves

8

3 Quart

temp-tations
presentable ovenware
by Tara

Maple Egg Biscuit Bake

I've always loved when the maple syrup from pancakes pools down onto my plate and into scrambled eggs—that is exactly what set me out to create this casserole recipe! With canned biscuits in place of pancakes, salty bacon to offset the sweet maple syrup, and brown sugar mixed right into the egg, this one dish is a full breakfast for 8, whipped up in minutes!

1. Preheat oven to 350 degrees. Spray a 3 quart temp-tations® baking dish with nonstick cooking spray.

2. Line the bottom of the baking dish with the canned biscuits, evenly spaced. Cover biscuits with the crumbled bacon.

3. In a large mixing bowl, whisk together remaining ingredients until eggs are scrambled and everything is well combined.

Shopping List

nonstick cooking spray

1 can **ready to bake biscuits**

½ pound **bacon**, cooked, and crumbled

8 large **eggs**, beaten

½ cup **milk**

¼ cup **maple syrup**

1 tablespoon **light brown sugar**

¼ teaspoon **salt**

4. Pour egg mixture over biscuits and bacon in baking dish and bake 30-35 minutes, or until edges are browned and the center is set. Let cool 5 minutes before serving.

tips by Tara

You can crumble and use pre-cooked bacon in this dish, but I would recommend microwaving for 1 minute to crisp up before adding to the casserole. If using pre-cooked, use 10 slices. Or try this with 1 cup of diced Canadian bacon!

brunch

Prep Time

10
mins

Cook Time

15
mins

Serves

4

1.5
Quart

temp-tations
presentable ovenware
by Tara

Veggie Frittata

This egg sensation is layered with hearty and nutritious broccoli, zucchini, peppers, and onions, and topped with mozzarella and Parmesan cheese. Once baked, this delicious and colorful dish is just right for brunch, lunch, or even a light supper. Serve with hash brown potatoes and crusty Italian bread.

1. Preheat oven to 425 degrees. Spray a 1.5 quart temp-tations® baking dish with nonstick cooking spray.

2. In a mixing bowl, beat eggs with salt and pepper.

3. In a skillet over medium heat, sauté the onion, bell pepper, broccoli, and squash in 2 tablespoons of the olive oil until crisp-tender, about 3 minutes.

4. Add the remaining tablespoon of olive oil to the vegetables in skillet, pour egg mixture over top, and add the basil. Cook 3-4 minutes, stirring occasionally, until eggs are softly scrambled.

Shopping List

nonstick cooking spray

8 large **eggs**

½ teaspoon **salt**

¼ teaspoon **black pepper**

3 tablespoons **olive oil**

½ cup chopped **yellow onion**

½ cup chopped **red bell pepper**

1 cup chopped **broccoli**

1 medium **yellow squash** or **zucchini**, sliced

½ teaspoon **dried basil**

½ cup shredded **mozzarella cheese**

¼ cup shredded or grated **Parmesan cheese**

5. Spoon cooked eggs and vegetables into the greased baking dish, top with both cheeses, and bake 10 minutes or until eggs are somewhat puffy. Serve hot.

tips by Tara

Soft scrambling the eggs with the vegetables keeps the veggies from settling at the bottom of the frittata. Leftovers will reheat perfectly in the microwave.

brunch

Deep Dish Blueberry Pancake

Fluffy, eggy, oven pancakes like this one are some of the most impressive breakfasts you can whip up. Though it does shrink some shortly after removing from the oven, it still settles at a nice size to feed the family!

brunch

1. Preheat oven to 425 degrees. Place butter in a 2.5 quart temp-tations® baking dish (round is best) and microwave for 15-20 seconds, just until melted. Shake dish from side to side to coat bottom and sides with the melted butter.

2. Whisk eggs until very frothy and then whisk in remaining ingredients, except blueberries, until very well combined and free of lumps.

Shopping List

2 tablespoons **butter** or **margarine**

5 eggs

1 cup **all purpose flour**

1 cup **milk**

2 teaspoons **vanilla extract**

3 tablespoons **sugar**

½ teaspoon **salt**

1 teaspoon **baking powder**

1 cup fresh **blueberries**

3. Pour the batter into the buttered baking dish and top with blueberries. Bake for 20-25 minutes or until fluffy and well browned around the edges. A toothpick inserted into the center should come out mostly clean. Serve immediately with powdered sugar, maple syrup, or both.

tips by Tara

Although the batter may seem thin, it is entirely normal for a fluffy oven pancake such as this. Substitute ½ cup of chocolate chips in place of the blueberries to make a Deep Dish Chocolate Chip Pancake!

shown in temp-tations® Old World 6 cup muffin pan

Banana Nut Muffins

Whenever I have bananas that are on the verge of turning brown, I usually place them in a food storage bag and freeze them for thawing out and making a few batches of muffins like these. Bananas tend to only get more flavorful as they turn brown, so don't throw them away, make muffins!

1. Preheat oven to 400 degrees. Spray a temp-tations® 6 cup muffin pan with nonstick cooking spray.

2. In a food processor, combine banana, butter, milk, egg, and vanilla extract, pulsing just until banana is finely chopped.

3. In a large bowl, combine all remaining ingredients, and then slowly fold in banana mixture until a batter is created.

4. Pour an equal amount of the batter into each of the 6 greased muffin cups. Bake 25-30 minutes, or until golden brown and a toothpick inserted into the center of one of the muffins comes out mostly clean.

Shopping List

nonstick cooking spray

1 large **banana**

3 tablespoons **butter** or **margarine**, softened

⅓ cup **milk**

1 large **egg**

¼ teaspoon **vanilla extract**

1 cup **all purpose flour**

⅓ cup **sugar**

1 teaspoon **baking powder**

¼ teaspoon **salt**

½ cup **chopped walnuts**

tips by Tara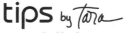

These are great served warm with a little bit of butter, at room temperature, or even chilled. Personally, I like to slice one in half and heat it in a hot, greased skillet until browned.

Baked Apple Cranberry Streusel

This versatile, make-ahead dish is a winner for brunch. I like to use a wide mixture of apples—tart apples like Granny Smith or Pippin, firm apples like Fuji or Golden Delicious, and sweet apples like Honeycrisp or Jonagold. Serve warm with ice cream or whipped cream, and you've got dessert.

1. Preheat oven to 350 degrees. In a 2.5 quart temp-tations® baking dish, make the filling by combining brown sugar, flour, cinnamon, and salt.

2. Add the cranberries and apples, and mix until the fruit is evenly coated in dry ingredients.

3. Make the topping by combining the flour, rolled oats, walnuts, brown sugar, and butter in the bowl of a food processor, and pulse until the mixture is crumbly, 1-2 minutes. Sprinkle evenly over the filling.

4. Bake 45 minutes or until apples are tender and the topping is golden brown. Cool 15-20 minutes before serving.

Shopping List

FILLING
¾ cup **light brown sugar**

¼ cup **all purpose flour**

1 teaspoon **cinnamon**

¼ teaspoon **salt**

½ cup **dried cranberries** (Craisins)

3 pounds **apples**, peeled and sliced

TOPPING
½ cup **all purpose flour**

½ cup **rolled oats**

½ cup **walnuts**

½ cup **light brown sugar**

1 stick **butter** or **margarine**, sliced

tips by Tara

Dried cherries or raisins can be substituted for the dried cranberries.

Prep Time
20 mins

Cook Time
8 mins

Serves
4

4 Quart

temp-tations
presentable ovenware
by Tara

brunch

Tuna Melt Bagels

Who doesn't love a tuna melt? This one is as good as the melts we remember from our childhood, only better because it's baked on chewy, hearty bagel halves. Serve with a green salad for a quick, satisfying supper or by itself for an easy weekend lunch.

1. Preheat oven to 400 degrees. In a medium mixing bowl, combine the tuna, relish, onion, celery, salt, and pepper.

2. Gently fold in mayonnaise, until evenly distributed.

3. Toast bagels and arrange the halves cut-side up in a 4-quart temp-tations® baking dish. Spread each bagel half with an equal amount of the tuna salad.

4. Top tuna salad on each bagel half with 1 slice of tomato and 1 slice of Swiss cheese. Bake 8-10 minutes or until the cheese is melted and gooey. Serve warm.

Shopping List

2 (7-ounce) cans **tuna packed in water**, drained

2 tablespoons **pickle relish**

2 tablespoons finely diced **yellow onion**

¼ cup finely chopped **celery**

½ teaspoon **salt**

¼ teaspoon **black pepper**

¼ cup **mayonnaise**, regular or reduced fat

4 **bagels**, split, thawed if frozen

1 large **tomato**, sliced

8 thin slices **Swiss cheese**

tips by Tara

Always check the can size of tuna because the contents can range from a full 7 ounces, all the way down to only 5 ounces. The less expensive cans of tuna may actually cost more per ounce! It's also very easy to replace the bagels in this dish with your favorite bread. Multi-grain or rye bread tastes especially delicious.

| shown on temp-tations® Old World fluted dessert plate

Prep Time

10
mins

Cook Time

22
mins

Serves

6

1.5
Quart

temp-tations
presentable ovenware
by Tara

brunch

Grandma Maria's Austrian Breakfast

This is my own foolproof version of my grandmother Maria's famous (in our house!) Austrian breakfast dish. Though she usually prepares these dense, eggy, and raisin filled Austrian pancakes on the stovetop, I've never quite been able to make them as good as hers. I can however whip together this oven baked version with much of the same spirit as her original! Serving alongside raspberry sauce or preserves, and topping with cinnamon and sugar is a must!

1. Preheat oven to 425 degrees. Spray a 1.5 quart temp-tations® baking dish with nonstick cooking spray.

2. In a large mixing bowl, whisk together melted butter, egg yolks, and milk. Add flour and baking powder, mixing until a thick batter is created.

3. In another mixing bowl, whisk egg whites and sugar until whites have nearly doubled in volume, about 2 minutes. (They do not have to be stiff like meringue, just visibly thicker.)

Shopping List

nonstick cooking spray

1 stick **butter** or **margarine**, melted

4 large **egg yolks**

¼ cup **milk**

1 ½ cups **all purpose flour**

½ teaspoon **baking powder**

4 large **egg whites**

⅓ cup **sugar**

½ cup **raisins**

4. Fold the egg white mixture into the flour mixture slowly, until both are combined. (Batter may be lumpy—that's okay.)

5. Fold raisins into the batter and then pour all into the greased baking dish. Bake 20-22 minutes, or until the top is well browned and the center is set. Serve hot, sprinkled with plenty of ground cinnamon and sugar, and alongside raspberry sauce or preserves for dipping.

tips by Tara

A mixture of golden and regular raisins can be used for a nice contrast. You can also top with confectioners sugar, but I prefer plain white granulated sugar.

Prep Time
15
mins

Cook Time
30
mins

Serves
16

3
Quart

temp-tations
presentable ovenware
by Tara

Homemade Granola Bars

You may have never thought of making your own granola bars, but let me tell you that it is well worth the effort! Choosing your own add-ins and how much of them that you would like to add is nice, but it's the fresh, homemade flavor that really sets these bars apart.

1. Preheat oven to 350 degrees and spray a 3 quart temp-tations® rectangular baking dish with nonstick cooking spray.

2. In a large bowl, whisk egg until frothy. Add brown sugar, butter, honey, and vanilla extract, and whisk all until completely smooth.

3. Whisk in flour, cinnamon, baking soda, and salt, until all are combined.

4. Using a wooden spoon, fold in oats, almonds, and raisins.

5. Spread mixture evenly across the bottom of the baking dish and cover with plastic wrap or aluminum foil. Press your hands over the plastic wrap to press the mixture down and even it out as best as you can. Remove plastic wrap and bake for 30 minutes, or until bars are beginning to brown.

6. Let cool completely before cutting into 16 bars. Cool uncovered and unrefrigerated so as to not create condensation. Bars are best stored individually wrapped at room temperature.

Shopping List

nonstick cooking spray

1 large **egg**

1 packed cup **light brown sugar**

¼ cup **butter** or **margarine**, softened

3 tablespoons **honey**

¾ teaspoon **vanilla extract**

1 cup **all purpose flour**

1 teaspoon **cinnamon**

½ teaspoon **baking soda**

⅓ teaspoon **salt**

3 cups **rolled oats**

½ cup **whole roasted almonds**, optional

½ cup **raisins**, optional

tips by Tara

You can make these with any dried fruit in place of the raisins, or no fruit at all. You can also try adding ½ cup of shredded coconut or even ½ cup of chocolate chips.

brunch

Turkey Club Casserole

One of my favorite things as a child was to go out for lunch with my parents and order my very own turkey club sandwich! The best part was the frilly toothpicks! This kid-friendly casserole has the same great flavors of the sandwich in a form that is large enough to feed the whole family. Though there isn't any reason to, you can still stick it with frilly toothpicks if you wish!

1. Preheat oven to 375 degrees. Spray a 2 quart temp-tations® baking dish with nonstick cooking spray.

2. Layer turkey at the bottom of the baking dish and then top with bacon. Top bacon with the sliced tomatoes.

3. In a medium mixing bowl, combine mayonnaise, Cheddar cheese, and mustard. Spread evenly over the tomatoes.

Shopping List

nonstick cooking spray

1 ½ pounds thick sliced **deli turkey breast**

12 slices **pre-cooked bacon**, each cut in half

2 tomatoes, sliced

½ cup **mayonnaise**, regular or reduced fat

1 cup shredded **Cheddar cheese**

2 teaspoons **mustard**

1 (**10** ounce) can refrigerated **buttermilk biscuits**

4. Separate biscuits and cut each into 2 pieces. Arrange biscuit pieces evenly over top of casserole.

5. Bake 20 minutes or until biscuits are golden brown. Cut into 6 pieces and serve.

tips by Tara

The only thing missing from this casserole is the lettuce, so be sure to serve alongside a green salad!

Poultry

Prep Time
20 mins

Cook Time
55 mins

Serves
4

4 Quart

temp-tations
presentable ovenware
by Tara

Chicken Cacciatore

This family style chicken dish is an Italian staple that can seem a little intimidating to make, but only until you get in there and actually make it! I make mine easy by "pan frying" the chicken with a high temperature bake in the oven before introducing the red sauce. Fresh sliced Roma tomatoes help conceal the use of store-bought red sauce.

1. Place chicken pieces in a large mixing bowl and cover with the flour, salt, pepper, and garlic powder. Toss to evenly coat all pieces with a thin layer of seasoned flour.

2. Preheat oven to 400 degrees. Place olive oil in a 4 quart temp-tations® baking dish, and bake in the preheated oven for 3 minutes, just to heat the oil. Add the floured chicken pieces to the hot oil in the baking dish, carefully flip to coat in oil, and bake for 20 minutes.

3. While the chicken is baking, add butter to a large skillet over medium-high heat. Once sizzling, add green bell pepper and onions. Sauté for 3 minutes before adding the mushrooms. Sauté all for about 5 minutes more, until mushrooms are almost tender.

4. Once the chicken has baked for 20 minutes, remove from oven and flip the pieces. Reduce oven temperature to 350 degrees. Combine marinara sauce, Roma tomatoes, and minced garlic with the sautéed vegetables in skillet, and then pour into the baking dish, surrounding the chicken.

5. Bake an additional 30-35 minutes, or until sauce is bubbling and cutting into a piece of chicken reveals juices that run clear. Serve hot with pasta and plenty of the sauce.

Shopping List

4 chicken breasts or **leg quarters**, bone-in and skin on

¼ cup **all purpose flour**

½ teaspoon **salt**

¼ teaspoon **black pepper**

¼ teaspoon **garlic powder**

3 tablespoons **olive oil**

1 tablespoon **butter** or **margarine**

1 green bell pepper, sliced into ¼ inch strips

1 small **red onion**, sliced thin

8 ounces sliced **button mushrooms**

1 jar (**24** ounces) **marinara sauce**

2 **Roma tomatoes**, sliced thin

2 teaspoons **minced garlic**

poultry

tips by Tara

When sautéing the mushrooms, it is best to use a very large skillet and spread them evenly throughout the pan. Let them cook without stirring for long intervals to give them time to brown.

Prep Time
15
mins

Cook Time
1
hour

Serves
8-10

3.5
Quart

temp-tations
presentable ovenware
by Tara

Lemon Roasted Chicken with Potatoes and Celery

A good roasted chicken cooked over potatoes has got to be the world's first "one dish meal". It's hard to improve too much upon something so classic, but I've always loved using a lot of fresh lemon when I roast chicken, as well as a little lemon pepper seasoning for even more bite.

1. Preheat oven to 400 degrees. Place all *Potatoes and Celery* ingredients into a 3.5 quart temp-tations® baking dish, and toss to combine and thoroughly coat.

2. Thoroughly drain chicken, remove any giblets and discard, and place atop the potato mixture in baking dish.

3. Rub all surfaces of the chicken's skin with the softened butter, squeeze lemon juice over top, and then sprinkle with the salt, pepper, and dill.

4. Bake 1 hour, basting once if desired, or until the drumstick moves freely in its socket and chicken juices run clear when pierced with a knife. Let rest for 10 minutes before carving. Serve with vegetables and plenty of juice from the baking dish.

Shopping List

POTATOES AND CELERY

4 ribs **celery,** cut into **2**-inch lengths

4 medium **potatoes,** peeled and cut into wedges

2 tablespoons **olive oil**

2 teaspoons **lemon pepper**

1 teaspoon **dried dill**

juice of **1 lemon**

CHICKEN

1 whole **chicken,** 4-6 pounds

3 tablespoons **butter** or **margarine,** softened

juice of **1 lemon**

½ teaspoon **salt**

¼ teaspoon **pepper**

½ teaspoon **dried dill**

poultry

tips *by Tara*

Russet potatoes, more commonly known as Idaho potatoes, contain the most starch of any variety so they cook up fluffy and absorb flavors well. However, if you'd like, you can use gold potatoes, which have a thin skin and do not require peeling to make this dish.

72 | shown in temp-tations® Toscana Rooster 2 quart covered baker

Chicken and Biscuits Casserole

When you are in the mood for a chicken pot pie, this dish really hits the spot without all of the labor of an actual chicken pot pie. With canned biscuits in place of a pie crust, it may actually taste better too! Who can resist fresh, hot, buttery biscuits? Leftover turkey is easily substituted in place of the chicken for a biscuit topped take on a turkey pot pie as well.

1. Preheat oven to 400 degrees.

2. Place butter, onion, and celery in a large skillet over medium high heat, sautéing until onions are translucent, about 4-5 minutes.

3. Add cream of chicken soup, milk, Parmesan cheese, poultry seasoning, black pepper, and frozen vegetables to the skillet and stir all to combine.

4. Combine chicken and flour in a large food storage container or bag and shake until chicken is thoroughly coated. Once mixture in the skillet is simmering, add in the coated chicken, stir, and let simmer 1 minute before removing from the heat.

Shopping List

2 tablespoons **butter** or **margarine**

½ cup diced **yellow onion**

¼ cup diced **celery**

2 cans **condensed cream of chicken soup**

2 cups **milk**

⅓ cup grated **Parmesan cheese**

¼ teaspoon **poultry seasoning**

⅛ teaspoon **black pepper**

1 ½ cups **frozen peas and carrots medley**

2 cups **cooked chicken**, diced

2 tablespoons **all purpose flour**

1 can **ready to bake biscuits**

5. Pour skillet mixture into a 2 quart temp-tations® baking dish and cover all with a single layer of uncooked biscuits. Bake all for 15-20 minutes, or until biscuits are golden brown and filling is hot and bubbly.

tips by Tara

Depending on the shape of the 2 quart dish you use, you may have more biscuits in the can than you can top the casserole with. If this is the case, simply bake the extra biscuits in another temp-tations® baking dish beside the casserole for anyone who wants seconds.

poultry

Chicken Caprese

This recipe reminds me of a tiny, beautiful island in Italy called Capri. The fresh, simple ingredients in this dish are readily available, even the jarred pesto, which was a real revelation the first time I purchased it. I like to serve this over pasta tossed in the remainder of the jar of pesto sauce mixed into a jar of Alfredo sauce.

poultry

1. Preheat the oven to 400 degrees. Spray a 3.5 quart temp-tations® baking dish with nonstick cooking spray.

2. In a mixing bowl, combine pesto sauce, salt, and pepper. Place tomato slices in bowl and gently toss to coat.

3. Arrange the breaded chicken in a single layer along the bottom of the greased baking dish.

4. Top the chicken with alternating slices of pesto coated tomato and mozzarella, and then drizzle with any remaining pesto from the mixing bowl.

5. Bake 10-15 minutes or until the chicken is hot throughout and mozzarella is melted and gooey. Serve garnished with fresh basil, if desired.

Shopping List

nonstick cooking spray

¼ cup **pesto sauce** (found near the spaghetti sauce)

¼ teaspoon **salt**

⅛ teaspoon **black pepper**

4 ripe **tomatoes**, sliced

2 pounds **breaded fully cooked chicken cutlets** or **patties**, defrosted

8 ounces fresh **mozzarella**, sliced

tips by Tara

Fresh mozzarella is usually sold in a large, baseball-sized ball in the imported cheese section of the deli, though they sometimes sell less expensive brands like Sargento in the regular cheese case. Shredded mozzarella can also be substituted. You can also start with frozen breaded chicken cutlets simply by baking according to package directions before preparing and only baking in step 5 until the cheese melts.

Prep Time	Cook Time		Serves	3.5
25 mins	**25** mins		**5**	**Quart**

temp-tations
presentable ovenware
by Tara

Chicken Enchiladas

Enchilada means tortillas "dipped in chili sauce" and has been enjoyed for countless years. This dish is a favorite in Mexican restaurants, often available in a myriad of different versions. In this recipe, I use softer flour tortillas instead of the usual corn. I also use boneless, skinless chicken thighs because they're so moist and juicy!

1. Preheat oven to 375 degrees. Heat oil in a nonstick skillet over medium to medium-high heat, and cook chicken 5 minutes on each side, or until the meat is firm and cutting into one reveals no pink. Remove from heat, cool and cut into strips.

2. In a mixing bowl, combine sliced chicken, onion, green bell pepper, 1 cup of the sour cream, 1 ½ cups of the cheese, 1 cup of the salsa, chili powder, oregano, salt, and pepper.

3. Spoon chicken mixture evenly into tortillas, rolling up and tucking in the sides of the tortillas. Spread 1 cup of the salsa across the bottom of a 3.5 quart temp-tations® baking dish. Arrange the enchiladas seam-side down over top.

Shopping List

1 tablespoon **vegetable oil**

2 pounds boneless, skinless **chicken thighs**

½ cup chopped **yellow onion**

½ cup chopped **green bell pepper**

1 ¼ cups **sour cream**, regular or reduced fat

2 cups shredded **Cheddar jack cheese**

3 cups **chunky salsa**

1 tablespoon **chili powder**

1 teaspoon **dried oregano**

½ teaspoon **salt**

¼ teaspoon **black pepper**

10 large **flour tortillas**

poultry

4. Cover with remaining salsa and remaining cheese. Spoon dollops of the remaining sour cream over top all. Bake 25 minutes, or until salsa is bubbling and cheese is beginning to brown. Let cool 5 minutes before serving.

tips by Tara

For a milder flavor, use only 1 cup salsa mixed with 2 cups of tomato sauce. Try using flavored tortillas, such as spinach or garlic, for more flavor, or use whole wheat tortillas to get more whole grains.

Prep Time

20
mins

Cook Time

43
mins

Serves

4

3

Quart

temp-tations
presentable ovenware
by Tara

Balsamic Glazed Chicken

This boneless, skinless chicken breast dish is on par with something you would be served in a nice restaurant, but is incredibly easy to make. The sweet and tangy balsamic sauce goes perfectly with the Italian herb rubbed chicken. Serve garnished with fresh herbs for the best presentation. Chop up some of those fresh herbs, and use about 1 tablespoon in place of the dried Italian seasoning for an even better flavor!

1. Place chicken, olive oil, Italian seasoning, garlic powder, salt, and pepper in a 3 quart temp-tations® baking dish and toss all to evenly coat chicken. Cover and refrigerate for 15 minutes to infuse the flavors.

2. Preheat the oven to 375 degrees. Create the sauce by placing olive oil and diced onion in a small sauce pan over medium heat, sautéing for 2-3 minutes, or until onions are translucent.

3. Add remaining *Sauce* ingredients to the saucepan and bring up to a simmer, simmering for 5 minutes, or until slightly thickened.

4. Pour sauce over seasoned chicken breasts in baking dish, and bake 30-35 minutes, or until cutting into a breast at the thickest part reveals no pink. Serve alongside your favorite vegetables and potatoes or pasta in red sauce.

Shopping List

4 boneless, skinless **chicken breasts**

1 tablespoon **olive oil**

½ teaspoon **Italian seasoning**

¼ teaspoon **garlic powder**

⅓ teaspoon **salt**

⅛ teaspoon **black pepper**

SAUCE

2 teaspoons **olive oil**

2 tablespoons finely diced **yellow onion**

¼ cup **balsamic vinegar**

1 tablespoon **light brown sugar**

1 tablespoon **Dijon mustard**

2 teaspoons **minced garlic**

poultry

tips by Tara

To make a meal like that shown in the photograph, bake thinly sliced bell pepper and a large bag of frozen potato wedges in a second rectangular temp-tations® baking dish alongside the chicken breasts, until potatoes are crispy. Transfer cooked chicken breasts to the dish of potatoes to serve.

Chicken and Wild Rice Casserole with Almonds

With a hint of curry, I make this creamy chicken and rice casserole with boxes of wild rice mix, as the wild rice cooks in less than half the time of starting from scratch. I like to make two distinct layers, one of creamy chicken in sauce, and another of the rice, but you can also just mix it all together before baking, if you prefer.

poultry

1. In a large pot over high heat, combine the chicken broth, curry powder, salt, and pepper. Add the chicken, cover, and bring to a boil. Reduce heat to medium-low and simmer 15 minutes or until the chicken meat is firm.

2. Add the onion and celery to the pot and cook 5 minutes longer.

3. Carefully remove chicken from the pot (reserving broth), and cool. Pull the meat from the bone and cut into strips or chunks. (It's okay if chicken is still pink, as it is going to be baked as well.)

4. Add the wild rice, butter, and 2 cups of water to the chicken broth, onions, and celery in the pot. Raise heat to high, stir well to combine, and bring to a boil. Reduce heat to medium-low, cover, and simmer 15 minutes, or until the rice has absorbed most of the water.

Shopping List

2 cups **chicken broth**

1 teaspoon **curry powder**

½ teaspoon **salt**

¼ teaspoon **black pepper**

3 pounds **chicken breasts**, bone-in

1 cup chopped **yellow onion**

1 cup chopped **celery**

2 (**6** ounce) packages **long grain and wild rice mix**, discard flavor packets

2 tablespoons **butter** or **margarine**

1 can (**10** ounces) **condensed cream of chicken soup**

¾ cup **sour cream**, regular or reduced fat

½ cup **sliced almonds**

5. Preheat oven to 350 degrees. Place the cooked chicken chunks in a 4 quart temp-tations® baking dish. Pour the soup and sour cream over top, mixing well to combine. Spread evenly throughout dish.

6. Spread the rice and any remaining cooking liquid over the chicken in baking dish and sprinkle with almonds. Bake 30 minutes, or until bubbling hot. Let cool 10 minutes before serving.

tips by *Tara*

If you don't like curry, replace it and the salt with 1 of the rice flavoring packets in step 1.

15 mins

2+ hours

8

Quart

temp-tations
presentable ovenware
by Tara

Herb Roasted Turkey Breast

Whole turkey breasts on the bone are usually available year round, can feed almost as many people as a whole turkey, and cook a lot faster than you might think. Rubbing the bird in homemade herb butter in this recipe is my take on a classic poultry preparation.

1. Preheat oven to 325 degrees. Place turkey breast in a 3.5 quart temp-tations® baking dish.

2. In a food processor, combine remaining ingredients, pulsing until herbs are chopped and distributed throughout butter.

3. Spread herb butter over turkey breast, covering all exposed skin. Bake uncovered for 90 minutes.

4. Tent turkey breast with aluminum foil and bake an additional 30-60 minutes, or until a meat thermometer inserted into the thickest part registers 185 degrees. Let turkey rest 10 minutes before carving.

Shopping List

1 turkey breast, bone-in, **5-7** pounds

4 tablespoons **butter** or **margarine**, softened

¼ cup **basil leaves**

⅓ cup **fresh parsley**

leaves of **2** sprigs of **thyme**

2 teaspoons **minced garlic**

2 teaspoons **lemon juice**

¼ teaspoon **poultry seasoning**

1 teaspoon **salt**

¼ teaspoon **black pepper**

poultry

tips by Tara

Check your grocer's refrigerated fresh herb section (near the produce) for a container of herbs labeled "bouquet" or "bouquet garni", as this one package contains many fresh herbs that work well here, saving you from having to purchase each herb separately.

Chicken, Tortellini, and Sundried Tomato Casserole

This quick and easy casserole features plump cheese tortellini and tangy sundried tomatoes in a creamy tomato "blush" or pink sauce. Using crushed croutons for the topping will give you a far coarser, crunchier top than Italian breadcrumbs, as those tend to be too fine.

1. Preheat oven to 350 degrees.

2. In a large pot, boil tortellini, undercooking by 2 minutes less than the package directions. Add sundried tomatoes to the pot in the last 2 minutes of cooking. Drain all and rinse under cold water.

3. Transfer drained tortellini and tomatoes to a 2.5 quart temp-tations® baking dish, and cover with all remaining ingredients, except crushed croutons. Toss all to combine.

4. Top casserole with crushed croutons and bake 15-20 minutes, or until hot and bubbly. Let cool 5 minutes before serving.

Shopping List

20 ounces **refrigerated cheese tortellini**

¾ cup sliced **sundried tomatoes**

1 ½ cups **cooked chicken**, cut into strips

2 cans **tomato bisque**

1 ¾ cups **milk**

¼ cup grated **Parmesan cheese**

¾ cup crushed **Italian seasoned croutons**

poultry

tips by Tara

The tortellini used in this recipe is the kind sold in the ordinary pasta aisle, though you can also use fresh, refrigerated tortellini or even frozen tortellini. There should be enough sauce to accommodate up to a 16 ounce package of tortellini, but I would recommend using a 3 quart baking dish in place of the 2.5 quart if using that much.

82 | shown in temp-tations® Old World 3.5 quart rectangular baker

Smothered Chicken Cordon Bleu

Chicken Cordon Bleu is one of my all time favorite dishes, though it is extremely difficult to make. My version doesn't require pounding the chicken flat, or stuffing with filling, but instead simply smothers the chicken with ham and cheese on top.

1. Preheat oven to 375 degrees. Spray a 3.5 quart temp-tations® baking dish with nonstick cooking spray.

2. Place breadcrumbs in a mixing bowl. In a separate mixing bowl, whisk together eggs, salt, and pepper. Dip chicken breasts in Italian breadcrumbs, then egg, and then back into bread crumbs, pressing down to fully coat on both sides. Place breaded chicken breasts in greased baking dish and bake 35 minutes.

3. While the chicken is baking, create the sauce by heating condensed soup and milk in a sauce pot over medium heat, just until hot and combined.

4. When the chicken is finished baking, top each breast with 1 slice of Swiss cheese and then cover with 1 folded slice of ham. Spoon 2 tablespoons of the sauce from the sauce pan over the center of each smothered breast. Reserve any remaining sauce, in case anyone would like extra on the side for dipping.

5. Bake an additional 5-10 minutes, or until cheese is melted and cutting into a breast at the thickest part reveals no pink. Serve alongside vegetables and rice or mashed potatoes.

Shopping List

nonstick cooking spray

1 ½ cups **Italian breadcrumbs**

2 large **eggs**

¼ teaspoon **salt**

⅛ teaspoon **black pepper**

4 boneless, skinless **chicken breasts**

1 can (**10** ounces) **condensed broccoli cheese soup**

¾ cup **milk**

4 slices **Swiss cheese**

4 slices **deli ham**

poultry

tips by Tara

I like to remove the chicken breasts from the dish in step 4 and add a large bag of frozen broccoli spears. Rinse the broccoli spears under hot running water to thaw beforehand. Once in dish, top the broccoli with the chicken and continue following the recipe, spooning extra sauce over the top of all.

Prep Time
15
mins

Cook Time
30
mins

Serves
6

3.5
Quart

(temp-tations)
presentable ovenware
by Tara

Chicken Noodle Casserole with Water Chestnuts

This family style casserole has a very unique twist... water chestnuts. Often overlooked, this crunchy and somewhat sweet vegetable is readily available in cans in the Asian foods aisle of the grocery store. For the easiest preparation, buy a can of sliced water chestnuts, rather than whole. If water chestnuts aren't your thing, you can always substitute 1 ½ cups of sliced carrots, sautéing them with the other vegetables in step 2.

poultry

1. Preheat oven to 350 degrees. Heat the vegetable oil in a medium skillet over medium to medium-high heat, and then cook chicken thighs 4 minutes on each side, or until firm. Transfer thighs to a cutting board, cool, and then cut into cubes.

2. Utilizing the same skillet, sauté the onion, bell pepper, and celery until crisp-tender, about 3 minutes.

3. Transfer the sautéed vegetables to a 3.5 quart temp-tations® baking dish. Cover with the diced chicken and all remaining ingredients, stirring well to combine.

Shopping List

2 tablespoons **vegetable oil**

1 ½ pounds boneless, skinless **chicken thighs**

½ cup chopped **yellow onion**

½ cup chopped **red bell pepper**

½ cup chopped **celery**

1 can (**8** ounces) **sliced water chestnuts**

1 can (**10** ounces) **cream of chicken soup**

1 cup **milk**

1 teaspoon **dried thyme**

½ teaspoon **salt**

¼ teaspoon **black pepper**

8 ounces **wide egg noodles**, cooked and drained

4. Bake 30 minutes or until bubbling hot. Let cool 5 minutes before serving.

tips by Tara

For even more color and more nutrition, add 1 cup of frozen edamame (tender green soybeans), frozen snow peas, or frozen peas in step 3. You can also top this casserole with Japanese Panko breadcrumbs (usually sold in the regular breadcrumb section, but sometimes in the Asian foods section) before baking for a nice crispy topping.

Hawaiian BBQ Chicken

If you've ever been lucky enough to visit the beautiful Hawaiian Islands, this chicken dish has the ability to bring back wonderful memories. With crushed pineapple, teriyaki sauce, honey, and ginger added to a traditional barbecue sauce, you're left with a flavor fit for a tropical paradise!

1. Preheat oven to 375 degrees. Arrange the chicken breasts, skin side up, in a 3.5 quart temp-tations® baking dish.

2. Pour the remaining ingredients over top, tossing with chicken to thoroughly coat each breast.

3. Bake 1 hour, or until sauce is bubbly, chicken is firm, and slicing into one breast reveals no pink. Serve drizzled in additional sauce from the baking dish.

Shopping List

4 chicken breasts, bone-in

1 cup **crushed pineapple**, with juice

1 cup **barbecue sauce**

¼ cup **teriyaki sauce**

¼ cup **honey**

1 teaspoon **ground ginger**

poultry

tips by Tara

Try using smoky chipotle flavored barbecue sauce here. Made from smoke-dried jalapeno peppers, chipotle chilis lend a wonderful flavor to sauces. Serve with rice and steamed vegetables like quick-cooking sugar snap peas. If you're serving six, this amount of sauce should be enough to cover 6 chicken breasts.

Ranch Chicken Casserole

This creamy casserole has all the great flavors of Ranch dressing that kids (and everyone!) love, along with rotini pasta, chicken, and a trio of colorful vegetables. I like to add a little bacon when I make it, but that's completely up to you! An absolute must is the cheese cracker topping—you can use Nips, Cheez-Its, or even Goldfish crackers.

1. Boil rotini pasta for 1 less minute than the package directions. Drain and rinse under cold water. Transfer to a 4 quart temp-tations® baking dish. (Rectangular is best.)

2. Preheat oven to 375 degrees. Place cream cheese, milk, butter, and Ranch dressing mix in a sauce pot over medium heat, stirring constantly until combined into a smooth sauce.

3. Pour sauce over rotini in the baking dish. Cover with chicken, carrots, corn, broccoli, and bacon pieces, and stir all until everything is equally coated in the sauce.

4. Top with the crumbled cheese crackers and bake for 20 minutes, just until bubbly hot. Let cool 5 minutes before serving.

Shopping List

16 ounces **rotini pasta**

8 ounces **cream cheese**, regular or reduced fat

2 ½ cups **milk**

3 tablespoons **butter** or **margarine**

1 packet (1 ounce) **powdered Ranch dressing mix**

1 pound **cooked chicken**, strips or cubed

1 cup **carrots**, frozen diced or fresh shoestring

1 cup **frozen corn kernels**

10 ounces **frozen broccoli florets**, thawed

½ cup **cooked bacon pieces**, optional

1 cup **cheese crackers**, crumbled

poultry

tips by Tara

I like to make this with the southwestern or fajita seasoned chicken breast strips that are sold pre-cooked near the lunch meats and also sold frozen in the frozen foods section of the grocery store. Just make sure to thaw the strips beforehand if using frozen.

Prep Time

Cook Time

Serves

4.

15
mins

10
mins

2

Quart

temp-tations
presentable ovenware
by Tara

Toasted Tuscan Turkey Subs

I am always thinking of new ways to use my bakeware, other than the usual casseroles and the like. These warm, toasted subs are most definitely something new, with turkey, provolone cheese, and an easy and delicious Italian artichoke spread in place of plain mayonnaise.

1. Preheat oven to 425 degrees. Slice sub rolls in half lengthwise and place all 4 halves in a large temp-tations® rectangular baking dish, crust sides down. A 4 quart dish works well, but you can also use a 5 quart or even a temp-tations® serving platter.

2. In a small bowl, combine mayonnaise, chopped artichoke hearts, Italian seasoning, and minced garlic. Microwave on high for 30 seconds, just until warmed.

3. Spread artichoke mixture on the 2 bottom sub halves, and then top with an even amount of the turkey breast. Top turkey breast with 2-3 large slices of tomato and 2 slices of red onion. The top halves of the sub roll should still be bare.

Shopping List

2 **6-8** inch **sub rolls**

¼ cup regular or reduced fat **mayonnaise**

½ cup **marinated artichoke hearts**, drained and chopped

¼ teaspoon **Italian seasoning**

1 teaspoon **minced garlic**

¾ pound deli sliced **turkey breast**

1 large **tomato**, sliced

4 thin slices **red onion**

4 slices **provolone cheese**

poultry

4. Place 2 slices of provolone on each of the top sub halves. Leave all 4 halves open faced and bake 6-10 minutes, just until cheese is bubbly and bread is beginning to brown around the edges.

5. Put the two subs together by situating the top halves onto the bottom halves. Serve immediately with potato chips or Greek Pasta Salad, recipe page: 19.

tips by Tara

Fresh sub rolls from the bakery section of the grocery store are best for these. You can also buy a longer loaf of bakery Italian bread and simply cut it into 2 sub rolls yourself.

Honey-Mustard Roasted Chicken and Sweet Potatoes

This recipe is so easy to do and EVER SO GOOD! With honey mustard smothered chicken baked right on top of a bed of sweet potatoes, the flavor combination is something different and sure to get you many rave reviews.

1. Heat oven to 425 degrees. Spray a 3.5 quart temp-tations® baking dish with nonstick cooking spray.

2. Place sweet potatoes at the bottom of the baking dish and top with sliced red onion.

3. Arrange the chicken pieces on top of onions, skin side up.

4. In a mixing bowl, combine honey mustard, vinegar, nutmeg, allspice, salt, and pepper, and pour over chicken in baking dish.

5. Cover with aluminum foil, bake 30 minutes, and then uncover and bake 30 minutes longer, or until the juices run clear when the chicken is pierced. Serve sweet potatoes and onions from bottom of dish alongside chicken.

Shopping List

nonstick cooking spray

4 medium **sweet potatoes**, peeled and cut into ¼ inch thick slices

1 medium **red onion**, sliced and separated into rings

4 chicken leg quarters or, **8 chicken thighs** or **drumsticks**

¾ cup prepared **honey mustard**

¼ cup **apple cider vinegar**

⅓ teaspoon **nutmeg**

¼ teaspoon **allspice**

½ teaspoon **salt**

¼ teaspoon **black pepper**

tips by Tara

It's quick and easy to make your own honey mustard, and you probably already have the ingredients in your pantry. Just combine ½ cup of prepared brown mustard with ¼ cup honey.

Meats

| shown transferred to a temp-tations® Old World serving platter

Prep Time

15
mins

Cook Time

22
mins

Serves

4

2.5
Quart

temp-tations
presentable ovenware
by Tara

Rosemary Pork Tenderloin

Pork tenderloin is one of the fastest cuts of meat you can roast. Extremely tender and lean, it may seem small, but it's all the good stuff! However, with such a quick cooking time, you have to be extra careful not to overcook it. I would definitely recommend using an electronic "probe" thermometer that you can leave in the meat as it roasts, setting the alarm for 160 degrees.

1. Preheat oven to 450 degrees. Spray a 2.5 quart temp-tations® rectangular baking dish with nonstick cooking spray.

Shopping List

nonstick cooking spray

1 pork tenderloin, 1 pound

1 ½ tablespoons chopped **fresh rosemary leaves**

1 tablespoon **olive oil**

1 tablespoon **minced garlic**

½ teaspoon **salt**

¼ teaspoon **black pepper**

2. Trim pork tenderloin of excess fat and place in the greased baking dish.

3. In a small bowl, combine remaining ingredients and then rub onto the entire surface of the tenderloin, pressing it down into the meat. Refrigerate for 30 minutes to marinate (optional, but recommended).

4. Bake 15-22 minutes, or until a thermometer inserted into the thickest part registers 160 degrees. Let cool at least 5 minutes before slicing.

tips by Tara

The key to this recipe is making sure that the rosemary leaves are very finely chopped, as they can actually get sharp as they roast. A spice mill works best for this, but it can also be done (carefully!) by knife.

meats

94 | shown transferred to a temp-tations® Old World serving platter

Deep Dish Pepperoni Pizza

This simple pizza can be thrown together in just a few minutes and is one of those great recipes to make as a family as the difficulty level is about as low as it gets!

1. Preheat oven to 425 degrees and spray a rectangular 4 quart temp-tations® baking dish with nonstick cooking spray. My 13x9 baker works best.

2. Unroll pizza crust and place at the bottom of the baking dish, stretching it to fill the entire bottom of the dish.

3. Spread pizza sauce over crust, and then top with ¾ of the mozzarella cheese. Arrange pepperoni slices and diced bell pepper over cheese.

Shopping List

nonstick cooking spray

1 can (**13.8** ounces) "classic" pizza crust (such as Pillsbury)

1 cup **pizza sauce**

2 cups **mozzarella cheese**

2 ounces sliced **pepperoni**

2 tablespoons diced **green bell pepper**, optional

1 tablespoon grated **Parmesan cheese**

4. Sprinkle remaining mozzarella cheese and grated Parmesan over top all, and bake for 20-25 minutes until crust is browned around the edges and cheese is bubbly. Let cool 5 minutes before cutting.

tips by Tara

Though pepperoni is always a hit with kids, you can use any of your favorite toppings in its place.

Diana's Pot Roast

My mother's best friend Diana was like a second mother to me. Sadly, she is no longer with us, but my family still prepares many of her amazingly original recipes, upholding some of her family traditions. This, her favorite pot roast recipe, is literally stuffed with a homemade onion stuffing.

1. Preheat oven to 350 degrees. Place vegetable oil in a large skillet over medium-high to high heat. Add roast to the skillet, season with the salt and pepper, and then brown well on all sides. Transfer browned roast to a 2.5 quart or larger temp-tations® baking dish.

2. Add sliced onions and 2 tablespoons of the butter to the same skillet the beef was browned in, and heat over medium-high heat, until onions caramelize. Add vodka and heat until simmering.

3. Pour the cooked onions and vodka over the roast in the baking dish, cover, and bake for 2 ½ hours, turning occasionally.

4. Place the remaining 2 tablespoons of butter in a temp-tations® mixing bowl and cover with chopped onion, bread crumbs, and parsley. Microwave for 1-2 minutes, just until butter is melted and combined.

5. Slice roast horizontally in ½ inch thick increments, being careful not to slice through to the bottom. Spoon bread crumb mixture evenly in between slices. Sprinkle flour over roast, and then pour beef broth over all. Bake an additional 30 minutes, or until meat is fork tender.

Shopping List

1 tablespoon **vegetable oil**
1 **bottom round roast, 3-5** pounds
2 teaspoons **salt**
½ teaspoon **black pepper**
1 cup sliced **onions**
4 tablespoons **butter**
½ cup **vodka** (may use water)
1 ½ cups chopped **onion**
½ cup **soft bread crumbs**
2 tablespoons **parsley**
1 tablespoon **all purpose flour**
1 cup **beef broth**

tips by Tara

Store bought stuffing can be used in place of making your own in step 4.

Prep Time	Cook Time		Serves	1
20 mins	**30** mins		**6**	**Quart**

temp-tations
presentable ovenware
by Tara

Bacon Cheeseburger Pie

Our favorite American standby, the cheeseburger is now all dressed up and ready to be served! Baked into a delicious, flaky crust, you can add a capital "C" to the word comfort! Go back in time to your favorite soda shop by serving alongside thick cut steak fries and an iceberg lettuce wedge salad with your favorite dressing.

1. Preheat oven to 375 degrees. Unroll pie crust and place in a 1 quart temp-tations® pie plate. Fold down and press top of crust into fluted edges of the pie plate.

2. In a large nonstick skillet, sauté ground beef, green bell pepper, and onion until meat is well browned. Remove from heat and drain thoroughly.

3. Add tomato sauce, chili sauce, Worcestershire sauce, salt, and pepper to drained beef mixture and stir to combine.

4. Pour mixture into prepared crust, top with bacon, and then cover all with the Cheddar cheese.

Shopping List

1 rolled **9 inch pie crust**, room temperature

1 pound **ground beef**

¼ cup chopped **green bell pepper**

¼ cup chopped **yellow onion**

½ cup **tomato sauce**

½ cup **chili sauce**

2 teaspoons **Worcestershire sauce**

½ teaspoon **salt**

¼ teaspoon **black pepper**

4 slices **pre-cooked bacon**, chopped

1 cup shredded **sharp Cheddar cheese**

5. Bake 30 minutes or until the crust has browned nicely and the cheese is beginning to brown. Cool pie 10 minutes before cutting into 6 slices.

tips by Tara

Ground turkey can be used in place of the beef, and the bacon can be left out entirely to make this lighter. You can also substitute the Cheddar with any shredded cheese. If you prefer American cheese, cut a second pie crust down to size and cover the entire top, pinching the pie closed, as American cheese tends to brown too quickly.

meats

Amy's Chili Mac

This kid (and adult!) friendly recipe by my best friend, Amy, is so easy to throw together, even though it starts with preparing your own homemade meat chili. If you've got an hour, you've got dinner… and probably a nice amount of leftovers for lunch the next day!

1. Boil elbow macaroni for 2 less minutes than the package directions. Drain and rinse under cold water. Transfer to a 4 quart temp-tations® baking dish. (Rectangular is best.)

2. Preheat oven to 375 degrees. Add ground beef and onions to a large nonstick skillet over medium-high heat to brown. Brown well, stirring constantly, about 10 minutes.

3. Add all remaining ingredients, except cheese, to the skillet and stir to combine.

4. Pour chili mixture in skillet over macaroni in baking dish and stir, until everything is completely incorporated. Cover with aluminum foil and bake 20 minutes.

5. Remove from oven, uncover, and top with Cheddar jack cheese. Return to oven and bake uncovered for an additional 15 minutes, or until cheese is very bubbly and beginning to brown. Let cool 5 minutes before serving.

Shopping List

16 ounces **elbow macaroni**

1 pound **lean ground beef**

1 cup diced **yellow onion**

1 can (**15** ounces) **kidney beans**, drained and rinsed

1 can (**6** ounces) **tomato paste**

2 cans (**10** ounces each) **diced tomatoes with green chilies**

1 ½ teaspoons **chili powder**

½ teaspoon **ground cumin**

1 teaspoon **salt**

½ teaspoon **garlic powder**

2 cups shredded **Cheddar jack cheese**

tips by Tara

If you are in a pinch, you can skip the skillet and make this a little less homemade by substituting 3 cans of chunky chili in place of everything but the macaroni and Cheddar jack cheese. Simply mix the chili into the macaroni right out of the can and continue the recipe as written.

meats

Prep Time
15
mins

Cook Time
4
hours

Serves
8

4
Quart

temp-tations
presentable ovenware
by Tara

Home-style Baked Corned Beef

Corned beef and cabbage is a classic in Ireland and elsewhere in Northern Europe where the winters are cold, and a hot dish of meat, potatoes, and vegetables helps the locals warm up. Often made in American slow cookers, this recipe slow roasts the beef in the oven, bringing out all kinds of wonderful flavors.

1. Preheat oven to 325 degrees. In a large pot, combine the beef broth, vinegar, and pickling spices. Bring to a boil, reduce heat, and simmer for 30 minutes to flavor the broth with the spices.

2. Strain the broth through a sieve into a 4 quart temp-tations® baking dish (It's okay if a few spices remain).

3. Place the corned beef in the baking dish, cover with aluminum foil, and bake 3 hours.

Shopping List

4 cups **low sodium beef broth** (can use ½ water)

1 cup **red wine vinegar**

3 tablespoons **pickling spices**

1 raw **corned beef brisket**, 3-5 pounds

1 small head **green cabbage**, quartered, each quarter cut in 3 wedges

1 ½ pounds small **red potatoes**

4 **carrots**, peeled and cut into 2 inch lengths

4. Uncover the baking dish and add the cabbage wedges, potatoes, and carrots. The cabbage may overfill the dish but will shrink down as it cooks. Re-cover and bake 1 hour longer, or until meat is fork tender.

5. Transfer beef to a cutting board and let rest for 10 minutes before slicing. Serve with vegetables from the baking dish and horseradish sauce or mustard, if desired.

tips by Tara

The pickling spices in this recipe can be replaced with a packet of pickling spices that usually comes along with the corned beef. Remember to always cut against the grain for the most tender meat.

meats

Sweet and Sour "Stuffed" Cabbage

The ultimate in homemade goodness, my version of "stuffed" cabbage is just as delicious as, and much easier than, the classic! The difference is that I make it in layers like lasagna, rather than painstakingly rolling cabbage leaves all day long.

1. Preheat oven to 325 degrees. In a large skillet over medium heat, brown the ground beef in the oil, crumbling it as it cooks. Add the chopped onions and cook 3 to 4 minutes longer, or until softened. Add the garlic, paprika, salt, and pepper, and stir to combine.

2. Remove ground beef mixture from heat and let cool at least 5 minutes before stirring in rice, eggs, and raisins.

3. Bring a large pot of salted water to a boil, add the cabbage, and cook 8 minutes or until soft. Drain through a colander and then run cold water over the leaves until cool enough to handle. Separate the cabbage leaves and trim off any tough ribs.

4. In a mixing bowl, combine the tomato sauce, brown sugar, and vinegar. Spread ⅓ of the sauce into the bottom of a 4 quart temp-tations® baking dish. Cover sauce in baking dish with ⅓ of the cabbage leaves and then ½ of the beef and rice mixture. Spread each layer evenly.

5. Make another layer of ⅓ of the sauce, then ⅓ of the cabbage, and then the remaining meat. Top with the remaining cabbage and then the remaining sauce. Cover dish with aluminum foil and bake 1 hour. Remove foil and bake 30 minutes longer, until browned and bubbly. Let cool 10 minutes before serving.

Shopping List

2 pounds **ground beef**

2 tablespoons **vegetable oil**

2 cups chopped **onions**

2 teaspoons **minced garlic**

2 teaspoons **paprika**

½ teaspoon **salt**

¼ teaspoon **pepper**

2 cups **cooked white rice**

2 large **eggs**, beaten

½ cup **raisins**, optional

1 medium head **cabbage**, cored

2 cups **tomato sauce**

½ cup **dark brown sugar**

2 tablespoons **apple cider vinegar**

meats

tips by Tara

This is really great with the raisins, especially if you use golden raisins, but they are not necessary if raisins and ground beef isn't your kind of thing!

Prep Time **10** mins

Cook Time **2** hours

Serves **10**

2.5 Quart

temp-tations
presentable ovenware
by Tara

Orange and Honey Glazed Ham

My grandmother always glazed our holiday hams with orange marmalade, as it gives the ham such a unique flavor. With not only orange marmalade, but honey and brown sugar as well, this ham cooks up with a brown, crispy, and sweet skin.

1. Preheat oven to 325 degrees.

2. Place ham in a 2.5 quart or larger temp-tations® baking dish.

3. In a small bowl, combine orange marmalade, honey, and mustard to create a glaze, and then spread over the entire surface of the ham.

4. Sprinkle brown sugar evenly over the glazed ham.

5. Bake for 1 ½ to 2 ½ hours, or until ham is warmed through.

Shopping List

1 ham, 5 to **10** pounds
½ cup **orange marmalade**
2 tablespoons **honey**
2 tablespoons prepared **brown mustard**
¼ cup **light brown sugar**

meats

tips by Tara

If glaze begins to burn before the ham is warmed through, loosely cover with aluminum foil for the remainder of the baking time.

Pork Chops with Apples and Raisins

You probably already know that pork and apples were most definitely meant to share the same plate, but you'd be surprised by what a few raisins can bring to the table! These sweet and savory chops are tops in my book, with just the right amount of brown mustard to spice things up.

1. Preheat oven to 350 degrees. Spread apples across the bottom of a 3.5 quart temp-tations® baking dish.

2. Sauté butter and onions in a pan over medium-high heat 5-7 minutes until onions cook down and are somewhat translucent.

3. Add apple juice, mustard, and raisins to onions, lower heat to medium, and simmer 5 minutes. Pour mixture over apples in baking dish.

4. Season both sides of pork chops with salt and pepper. Add oil and chops to a large skillet over medium-high heat and brown lightly on both sides, about 3-4 minutes per side. Arrange chops on top of apples. Cover and bake for 40-45 minutes, until pork chops are tender.

5. Serve pork chops smothered in the stewed apples, raisins, onions, and liquid from the pan. Pair with my Green Beans Almondine, recipe page: 151, for a full meal!

Shopping List

3 large **red apples**, peeled, cored and cut into ½ inch wedges

2 tablespoons **butter**

1 small **yellow onion**, peeled and sliced into ¼ inch rings

1 ½ cups **apple juice**

3 tablespoons **brown mustard**

½ cup **raisins**

6 **pork chops**, about ¾ inch thick

½ teaspoon **salt**

¼ teaspoon **pepper**

1 tablespoon **vegetable oil**

tips by Tara

While sautéing the onions, simmering the sauce, and browning the pork chops before baking adds additional flavor and color, this will still come out delicious by assembling all ingredients raw. Just add an additional 10 minutes to the baking time.

Prep Time	Cook Time		Serves	2.5
15 mins	**30** mins		**6**	**Quart**

temp-tations
presentable ovenware
by Tara

Southwestern Cottage Pie

Cottage pie is a delicious comfort food that dates back to the late 1700's, originating in the beautiful countryside of England. Today, I've added peppers, onions, corn, and spicy pepper jack cheese to give it a fun Southwestern twist!

1. Preheat oven to 350 degrees. Spray a 2.5 quart temp-tations® baking dish with nonstick cooking spray.

2. Place oil in a large nonstick skillet over medium-high to high heat and sauté the onion and red and green bell peppers until softened, about 3 minutes. Add ground beef and cook until the beef is well browned.

3. Stir in the flour, mixing well to combine, and then add salsa, corn, salt, and pepper. Stir constantly, until mixture is simmering and then pour into the greased baking dish.

4. In a large mixing bowl, combine mashed potatoes with sour cream and spread evenly over ground beef mixture in baking dish. Top all with pepper jack cheese and bake for 30 minutes, until hot and bubbly. Let cool 5 minutes before serving.

Shopping List

nonstick cooking spray

2 tablespoons **vegetable oil**

1 cup chopped **onion**

½ cup chopped **red bell pepper**

½ cup chopped **green bell pepper**

1 ½ pounds **ground beef**

2 tablespoons **flour**

1 cup **salsa**

1 cup **frozen corn kernels**

½ teaspoon **salt**

¼ teaspoon **black pepper**

3 to 4 cups warm **mashed potatoes**

½ cup **sour cream**, regular or reduced fat

1 cup shredded **pepper jack cheese**

meats

tips by Tara

Frozen onion and bell pepper stir fry medleys can be substituted for the fresh onions and peppers in the recipe. Also, instant mashed potatoes prepared according to the package directions work just fine for the potatoes in this. For a milder flavor, shredded Colby jack or Cheddar jack cheese can be used in place of the pepper jack.

| shown transferred to a temp-tations® Old World oval serving platter

Prep Time **10** mins

Cook Time **35** mins

Serves **6**

2 Quart

temp-tations
presentable ovenware
by Tara

Corn Dog Casserole

Making corn dogs at home isn't exactly an easy task and making them without deep frying them is all but impossible. Even frozen corn dogs that you can bake at home are fried before freezing, so I really like that this recipe gets around the need for frying by baking the hotdogs directly in a moist and sweet cornbread!

1. Preheat oven to 400 degrees. Place butter in a 2 quart temp-tations® baking dish and microwave for 15-20 seconds, just until melted. Shake dish from side to side to coat bottom and sides with the melted butter.

2. Place the muffin mix, eggs, and milk into a large temp-tations® mixing bowl and mix until a well combined batter is created.

3. Pour ⅓ of the batter into the greased 2 quart baking dish and then place whole hotdogs in rows over top, about ¾ inch apart. To extend each row to about ½ inch from the edge of the dish on either side, you will most likely need to cut 2 of the hotdogs into smaller pieces to add in.

4. Place 4 slices of American cheese evenly over the hotdogs, and then cover all with the remaining ⅔ of the batter. Bake for 30-35 minutes, until the top has browned well and a toothpick inserted into the center comes out clean of any batter. Let cool 5 minutes before slicing. Serve with ketchup or mustard, as you would eat an ordinary corn dog.

Shopping List

1 tablespoon **butter** or **margarine**
2 boxes (8.5 ounces each) **corn muffin mix**
2 large **eggs**
¾ cup **milk**
6-8 **hotdogs** or **turkey franks**
1 tablespoon **sugar**
4 slices **American cheese**, optional

tips by Tara

Though the cheese really adds a lot to this recipe, it is not entirely necessary, as there isn't any cheese in an ordinary corn dog!

Prep Time	Cook Time		Serves	2.5
20 mins	**3** hours		**8**	Quart

temp-tations
presentable ovenware
by Tara

Mom's Sweet and Sour Pot Roast

This is my mother's favorite way to prepare pot roast—it also happens to be just about the easiest way to prepare one that is full of flavor. The cranberry sauce adds a sweet and tangy bite, and the onion soup mix adds a whole bunch of different flavors in one simple ingredient! Serve alongside your favorite vegetables or add them directly to the baking dish in the last hour of baking.

1. Preheat oven to 325 degrees.

2. Place vegetable oil in a large skillet over medium-high to high heat. Add roast to the skillet and brown well on all sides. Transfer browned roast to a 2.5 quart or larger temptations® baking dish.

Shopping List

1 tablespoon **vegetable oil**

1 **bottom round roast, 3-5** pounds

½ cup **dry red wine** (may use beef broth)

1 packet **powdered onion soup mix**

1 can **jellied cranberry sauce**

2 rounded teaspoons **minced garlic**

3. Add remaining ingredients to the same skillet the beef was browned in and heat over medium heat, stirring constantly, just until cranberry sauce melts. Scrape the bottom of the skillet to break up any browned bits of the beef to add to the sauce.

4. Pour the sauce over the roast in the baking dish, cover, and bake for 2 ½ to 3 hours, or until meat is fork tender.

tips by Tara

If you let the roast sit for 5 minutes after baking, you can skim any excess grease off of the top of the juices in the baking dish. Once you've done that, slice or shred the roast and serve drizzled in plenty of the juices from the dish.

Meat Lover's Lasagna

I make this chunky, meaty lasagna whenever I have a crowd to feed. It's filling and everyone from young to old loves it. Using Italian sausage as well as ground beef in the sauce adds a ton of extra flavor. Just be sure to buy bulk Italian sausage (which looks like ground beef), or to slice and remove the casings if links are all you can find.

1. In a large skillet over medium-high heat, brown the ground beef and sausage in olive oil, about 5 minutes, crumbling them as they cook. Drain any excess grease and then add onions and garlic, sautéing until onions are translucent, about 3 minutes.

2. Lower heat to low, add marinara sauce and simmer 25-30 minutes, stirring occasionally, or until the sauce is nice and thick.

3. Preheat oven to 350 degrees. In a mixing bowl, combine ricotta cheese, eggs, ½ cup of the Parmesan cheese, 1 cup of the mozzarella cheese, Italian seasoning, salt, and pepper.

4. Spoon a thin layer of sauce into the bottom of a 4 quart temp-tations® baking dish. Cover with a layer of lasagna noodles, using about ¼ of the noodles. Spoon ½ of the ricotta mixture over top. Cover with a layer of ¼ more of the noodles, and then spoon ⅓ of the remaining meat sauce over top. Repeat one more time.

Shopping List

1 pound **ground beef**

1 pound **bulk Italian sausage**

2 tablespoons **olive oil**

1 cup chopped **yellow onion**

2 teaspoons **minced garlic**

5 cups jarred **marinara sauce**

32 ounces **part skim ricotta cheese**

4 **eggs**, beaten

¾ cup grated **Parmesan cheese**

2 ½ cups shredded **mozzarella cheese**

½ teaspoon **Italian seasoning**

½ teaspoon **salt**

¼ teaspoon **black pepper**

16 ounces **lasagna noodles**, boiled **8** minutes

5. Finish by covering the top noodles with any remaining sauce and the remaining Parmesan and mozzarella cheese. Bake 1 hour or until the sauce is bubbly and the top is browned. Cool 15 minutes before slicing.

tips by Tara

You can also substitute ground turkey and turkey sausage in place of the ground beef and Italian sausage for a lighter dish.

Family Favorite Meatloaf

A nice loaf pan was one of my most requested dishes, and that was due in no small part to a favorite amongst almost all families—meatloaf. This recipe doesn't shy too far from the classic that we all grew up with, but is specifically written as the perfect fit for my 1.7 quart loaf pan to eliminate any guesswork.

1. Preheat oven to 350 degrees and spray a 1.7 quart temp-tations® loaf pan with nonstick cooking spray.

2. In a large bowl, mix the ground beef, milk, ketchup, breadcrumbs, yellow onion, eggs, Parmesan cheese, salt, and pepper.

3. Evenly fill loaf pan with the meatloaf mixture, patting with your hands to form an even top. Bake uncovered for 30 minutes.

4. In a small bowl, combine the *Topping* ingredients.

5. Remove loaf from oven, drain any excess fat, and spread the topping over loaf evenly. Return to oven and bake an additional 45 minutes, or until a meat thermometer registers 165 degrees. Drain any additional fat from pan and let rest 10 minutes before cutting into 8 equal slices.

Shopping List

nonstick cooking spray
2 pounds **lean ground beef**
⅓ cup **milk**
¼ cup **ketchup**
¾ cup **Italian breadcrumbs**
¼ cup minced **yellow onion**
2 large **eggs**
⅓ cup grated **Parmesan cheese**
¾ teaspoon **salt**
¼ teaspoon **pepper**
TOPPING
½ cup **ketchup**
1 tablespoon **dark brown sugar**
1 teaspoon **Worcestershire sauce**

tips by *Tara*

You can also bake this in any of my large rectangular baking dishes by simply forming into a thick, oval loaf in the center of the dish.

meats

| shown in temp-tations® Old World Embossed 3 quart rectangular baker

Spice-Rubbed Baby Back Ribs

Smaller and leaner, baby back ribs are definitely the prime cut of ribs. I like to cut the ribs into smaller sections for easy serving, and then coat with a dry rub of great flavors before topping with barbecue sauce. Just be sure to serve with plenty of napkins!

1. Preheat oven to 325 degrees. Cut ribs into 2-rib sections. (This is easiest to do by cutting in between the ribs from the larger end of the rib toward the smaller end.)

2. In a mixing bowl, combine chili powder, paprika, cumin, oregano, salt, and pepper, and rub over all sections of the ribs.

3. Arrange rib sections in a 3 quart or larger temp-tations® baking dish. Cover with aluminum foil and bake 3 hours, or until the meat is fork tender and the ribs are well-browned.

Shopping List

1 rack **baby back ribs, 4-5** pounds
1 tablespoon **chili powder**
1 tablespoon **paprika**
1 teaspoon **ground cumin**
1 teaspoon **oregano**
½ teaspoon **salt**
¼ teaspoon **black pepper**
1 cup **barbecue sauce**

4. Raise oven temperature to 400 degrees. Drain any grease from the baking dish. Cover all ribs in the barbecue sauce, tossing to ensure that they are evenly coated.

5. Bake 30 more minutes, or until the barbecue sauce has turned into a nice glaze. Serve hot, topped with additional barbecue sauce, if you desire.

tips by Tara

Heat any additional barbecue sauce in the microwave for about 1 minute before topping the ribs when serving to ensure that everything is nice and hot!

meats

Prep Time	Cook Time		Serves	2.5
20 mins	**1** hour		**6**	**Quart**

temp-tations
presentable ovenware
by Tara

"Dad's Favorite" Scotch Hash

Many nationalities have a version of this simple and tasty ground beef dish that is similar to a ground beef stroganoff. This is my father's favorite recipe, with a slight kick from curry powder that infuses into the meat as it bakes.

1. Preheat oven to 300 degrees.

2. In a large skillet over medium-high heat, sauté ground beef, curry powder, salt, and pepper until beef is almost entirely browned.

3. Add onions and continue cooking until onions are translucent.

4. Sprinkle flour over top and then pour in beef broth. Stir all to combine.

5. Transfer to a 2.5 quart temp-tations® baking dish and bake for 55-60 minutes, or until bubbly and thickened.

Shopping List

2 pounds **ground beef**

1 teaspoon **curry powder**

¾ teaspoon **salt**

⅛ teaspoon **pepper**

1 large **onion**, thinly sliced

¼ cup **all purpose flour**

2 cups **beef broth**

tips by Tara

This is great served over mashed potatoes or noodles, especially broad noodles, such as egg noodles.

meats

Seafood

Basil Pesto Salmon

I love pesto sauce and use it in several recipes throughout this book. This quick and easy Basil Pesto Salmon includes a recipe for homemade pesto sauce in case you want to use it in other recipes in this book. Of course, you can also substitute a small jar of store bought pesto sauce to make this even quicker.

1. Preheat oven to 400 degrees. Place squash, tomatoes, olive oil, garlic powder, salt, and pepper in a 3 quart temp-tations® baking dish and toss all to coat.

2. Place salmon fillets over vegetables in baking dish and squeeze lemon juice over all.

3. In a food processor, combine all *Pesto* ingredients, pulsing until a fine paste is created.

4. Spread pesto sauce evenly over the top of the salmon fillets. Bake 15-20 minutes, or until salmon is flaky and vegetables are tender. Serve immediately.

Shopping List

4 cups sliced **yellow squash**

8 ounces **cherry tomatoes**

2 tablespoons **olive oil**

⅛ teaspoon **garlic powder**

½ teaspoon **salt**

¼ teaspoon **black pepper**

4 portions **salmon fillets**, about **1 ½** pounds, skinless

juice of ½ **lemon**

PESTO

1 packed cup **basil leaves**

¼ cup grated **Parmesan cheese**

¼ cup **pine nuts**

3 tablespoons **olive oil**

¼ teaspoon **salt**

seafood

tips by Tara

When purchasing fresh salmon, don't be afraid to ask your grocer's seafood department to cut the salmon from the skin for you. Of course, they'll probably weigh it and print up a pricing label before removing!

Prep Time
20 mins

Cook Time
35 mins

Serves
4

2 Quart

temp-tations
presentable ovenware
by Tara

Greek Shrimp and Feta Casserole

Covering and baking shrimp dishes like this one is a great way to infuse flavors, not only into the shrimp, but the flavor of the shrimp into the pasta and other ingredients as well. Here, I use the great Greek flavors of tomato, oregano, lemon, and feta cheese to complement the shrimp. A nice, thick spaghetti works best for this dish.

1. Preheat oven to 375 degrees.

2. In a large pot, boil spaghetti in lightly salted water, undercooking by 2 minutes less than the package directions. Drain well.

3. Transfer drained spaghetti to a 2 quart temp-tations® baking dish and cover with all remaining ingredients, except feta cheese. Toss all to combine.

4. Top casserole with feta cheese, cover dish with aluminum foil, and bake 30-35 minutes, or until shrimp are pink and white throughout. Let cool 5 minutes before serving.

Shopping List

8 ounces **spaghetti**

1 pound **shrimp**, peeled and deveined

1 large **tomato**, chopped

4 tablespoons **butter** or **margarine**, melted

juice of **1 lemon**

2 teaspoons **minced garlic**

½ teaspoon **dried oregano**

¾ teaspoon **salt**

¼ teaspoon **pepper**

½ cup crumbled **feta cheese**

tips by Tara

You can also add a 10 ounce package of chopped spinach to the casserole in step 3 for an all-in-one meal. Thaw and squeeze the water from the spinach before adding for best results.

seafood

Baked Buttermilk Scallops

Buttermilk is a cook's best friend in the kitchen, because it helps keep foods juicy and tender as it does in this quick Cape Cod style scallop dish. Though available year-round, scallops are at their best in fall and winter. The bigger the scallop, the better, as they'll cook up nice and meaty!

1. Preheat oven to 400 degrees. Arrange the scallops in a single layer along the bottom of a 2.5 quart rectangular temp-tations® baking dish.

2. Pour the buttermilk over top scallops, and then add the salt, Italian seasoning, and lemon pepper, tossing to combine. (Though it doesn't seem like a lot of liquid, the scallops will give off their own juices in baking.)

3. Sprinkle with cracker crumbs and drizzle with melted butter.

Shopping List

2 pounds **sea scallops,** any hard muscle pieces at the side removed

½ cup **buttermilk**

½ teaspoon **salt**

1 teaspoon **Italian seasoning**

1 teaspoon **lemon pepper**

1 cup crushed **crackers**

4 tablespoons **butter** or **margarine,** melted

1 lemon, cut into wedges

4. Bake 20 minutes, or until the scallops are opaque and the cracker crumbs are browned. Serve immediately with a wedge of lemon over steamed rice to soak up the delicious juices from the baking dish.

tips by Tara

If you use frozen scallops, defrost overnight in the refrigerator so they don't lose their natural juices. Drain well and pat dry before cooking. Sea scallops (the larger scallops) work best here; small bay scallops would get too rubbery. I prefer a plain white cracker for the crumbs, such as oyster crackers or Saltines.

seafood

Prep Time
20 mins

Cook Time
25 mins

Serves
4

3 Quart

temp-tations
presentable ovenware
by Tara

Crispy Tilapia with Lemon

These crunchy breaded tilapia fillets are amazingly delicious when you squeeze lemon juice over them right before eating. Served over a bed of zucchini and onions, you can also make this without the vegetables if you prefer. Just be sure to spray the dish with nonstick cooking spray and watch the fish carefully, as they will cook faster when they are not sitting on vegetables and have direct contact with the baking dish.

1. Preheat oven to 400 degrees.

2. Place all *Vegetables* ingredients into a 3 quart temp-tations® baking dish and toss to combine.

3. In a large bowl, combine breadcrumbs, Italian seasoning, and Parmesan cheese. Dip tilapia fillets into the melted butter and then into the bowl of seasoned breadcrumbs, tossing to fully coat.

4. Place breaded tilapia fillets over the vegetables in the baking dish, and sprinkle each with a pinch of salt and pepper. Pour any remaining butter over all in the baking dish, including the vegetables.

5. Bake 20-25 minutes, or until tilapia is crunchy on the outside and flaky on the inside. Serve with plenty of lemon wedges to squeeze over fish.

Shopping List

VEGETABLES (OPTIONAL)
1 tablespoon **olive oil**
4 cups sliced **zucchini**
1 small **yellow onion**, sliced
¼ cup diced **red bell pepper**
½ teaspoon **salt**
⅛ teaspoon **black pepper**

TILAPIA
1 ½ cups **Panko breadcrumbs**
1 teaspoon **Italian seasoning**
3 tablespoons grated **Parmesan cheese**
1 ½ pounds **tilapia fillets**
4 tablespoons **butter**, melted
salt and **pepper**
lemon wedges

seafood

tips by Tara

Progresso makes Italian seasoned Panko breadcrumbs that work even better in this recipe… simply skip the Italian seasoning in step 3 if you are using them. (I would still use the Parmesan cheese, as it makes just about everything taste better!)

Southern Style Tuna Noodle Casserole

This recipe is a family favorite; an easy basic casserole I've been making for years with a Southern style spin of pimento, paprika, and hot sauce. You can easily prepare it ahead of time, as long you mix up the topping right before baking to ensure that it stays crunchy.

1. Preheat oven to 350 degrees. In a large skillet over medium-high heat, melt butter and then sauté onion, celery, and mushrooms until tender, about 5 minutes. Stir in cream of mushroom soup, milk, choppped pimento, and hot sauce, and then remove the skillet from the heat.

2. Place egg noodles and tuna (with liquid from can) in a 2.5 quart temp-tations® baking dish. Cover with sautéed vegetable and sauce mixture from the skillet and stir all to combine.

3. In a small bowl, combine *Topping* ingredients and sprinkle over casserole.

4. Bake 25-30 minutes or until hot, bubbly, and lightly browned. Serve immediately.

Shopping List

2 tablespoons **butter** or **margarine**

¼ cup chopped **yellow onion**

½ cup chopped **celery**

8 ounces sliced **mushrooms**

1 can **condensed cream of mushroom soup**

1 ¼ cups **milk**

2 tablespoons chopped **pimento**

1 teaspoon **hot sauce**

8 ounces **egg noodles**, cooked and drained

1 (7 ounce) can **tuna packed in water**

TOPPING

½ cup **cracker crumbs**

1 teaspoon **paprika**

2 tablespoons **butter** or **margarine**, melted

tips by Tara

Roasted red peppers (sold in jars near the olives) can be used in place of the chopped pimento, and 2 cups of cooked chicken or turkey can be used in place of the tuna.

seafood

Almond-Crusted Tilapia

In the past, frozen fish wasn't very good quality, but in the last five years or so, freezing technology has greatly improved and now fish are cleaned and filleted on board the same ships they're caught on. These "frozen at sea" fish are sometimes even fresher than actual fresh fish. Just be sure to defrost overnight in the refrigerator to keep the fish nice and juicy. With a nice crunch from sliced almonds, this recipe for tilapia is light and delicious.

1. Preheat oven to 425 degrees. Spray a 3.5 quart temp-tations® baking dish with nonstick cooking spray. Arrange the tilapia fillets along the bottom of the baking dish.

2. Drizzle tilapia with olive oil and lemon juice and then sprinkle with lemon pepper, dill, and salt.

3. Cover each fillet with the almonds, pressing them down into the flesh of the fish to stick.

Shopping List

nonstick cooking spray

4 portions (about **1 ½** pounds) **tilapia fillets**, defrosted if frozen

2 tablespoons **olive oil**

juice of **1 lemon**

2 teaspoons **lemon pepper seasoning**

1 teaspoon **dried dill**

½ teaspoon **salt**

¼ cup **sliced almonds**

seafood

4. Bake 15 minutes, or until the tilapia flakes and almonds are browned. Serve drizzled in juices from the baking dish.

tips by Tara

You can use this same recipe for salmon, flounder, or catfish fillets. Using fresh chopped dill in place of the dried is even more delicious. Use at least 2 teaspoons of the fresh chopped in place of the dried, if you can.

Prep Time
30 mins

Cook Time
8 mins

Serves
6

2.5 Quart

temp-tations
presentable ovenware
by Tara

Cajun Shrimp

This tasty and quick shrimp sauté is typical of Southern Louisiana's distinctive Cajun cooking. With spicy and robust Cajun seasoning (sold in many varieties in the spice aisle of the grocery store) and tons of diced tomatoes that cook into a chunky sauce, be sure to serve over rice to soak up all the flavor.

1. In a large mixing bowl, combine Cajun seasoning, lemon juice, and Worcestershire sauce. Add shrimp and toss to coat. Place in refrigerator and marinate for just 15 minutes. (Any longer and the lemon juice will actually start to cook the shrimp.)

2. Melt butter in a large nonstick skillet over medium heat. Add garlic and sauté until fragrant, about 2 minutes.

3. Remove shrimp from marinade and transfer to the skillet. Add diced tomatoes and cook shrimp for about 3 minutes on each side, or until the shrimp are opaque and the tomatoes are bubbling.

4. Transfer all to a 2.5 quart temp-tations® baking dish to serve hot. Serve over steamed white or yellow rice cooked according to package directions.

Shopping List

2 tablespoons **Cajun seasoning**

juice of **2 lemons**

1 tablespoon **Worcestershire sauce**

2 pounds **extra-large shrimp** (**16** to **20** per pound), peeled and cleaned

4 tablespoons **butter** or **margarine**

1 tablespoon **minced garlic**

2 cups diced **tomatoes**, fresh or drained canned

tips by Tara

For a less spicy dish, you can substitute milder Old Bay seasoning. Use the largest shrimp you can buy because they're meatier and won't overcook and toughen. If you purchase frozen shrimp, defrost in the refrigerator overnight to ensure that the shrimp stay plump and juicy.

seafood

Pasta / Rice

126 | shown in temp-tations® Old World 2 quart square baker

Traditional Baked Macaroni and Cheese

I usually start my macaroni and cheese on the stove, but one day I was interested in trying it the old fashioned way, starting with dry, uncooked pasta. I can tell you that I was pleasantly surprised by how much flavor cooks right into the macaroni as it bakes surrounded by milk and cheese. It does take a little longer to bake, but it's also time you've saved by skipping the stove.

1. Preheat oven to 375 degrees. Place butter in a 2 quart temp-tations® baking dish and microwave for 15-20 seconds, just until melted. Shake dish from side to side to coat bottom and sides with the melted butter.

2. Place the cornstarch and ¾ of the Cheddar cheese (reserving the rest to top the casserole later) into a large temp-tations® mixing bowl and toss until cheese is coated.

Shopping List

2 tablespoons **butter** or **margarine**

2 teaspoons **cornstarch**

2 cups shredded **sharp Cheddar cheese**

8 ounces **uncooked elbow macaroni**

2 ½ cups **milk**

½ teaspoon **dry mustard**

½ teaspoon **salt**

3. Add remaining ingredients to the mixing bowl and stir well. Pour mixture into the greased 2 quart temp-tations® baking dish, cover with aluminum foil, and bake for 40 minutes.

4. Remove dish from oven, uncover, and stir well. Top with remaining Cheddar cheese and return to the oven, uncovered. Bake an additional 25-30 minutes, until cheese on top is very well browned. Let rest 10 minutes before serving.

tips by Tara

While it may seem strange to start by tossing the shredded cheese with cornstarch, this is how most cheese fondues are started and helps the cheese stay thick and creamy as it melts.

pasta/rice

| shown in temp-tations® Old World 4 quart (13x9) rectangular baker

Prep Time	Cook Time		Serves	4
20 mins	**45** mins		**8**	**Quart**

temp-tations
presentable ovenware
by Tara

Baked Three Cheese Spaghetti

Baked spaghetti has always been a favorite of mine as the flavors really bake together in a way that you just can't get from simply topping pasta with sauce off of the stove. My recipe is loaded with three cheeses—ricotta, Parmesan, and mozzarella. If you prefer your baked spaghetti with meat sauce, simply follow my tip at the bottom of the page!

1. Preheat oven to 350 degrees. Boil spaghetti for 2 less minutes than the package directions. Drain and rinse under cold water. Transfer to a 4 quart temp-tations® baking dish. (Rectangular is best.)

2. Add ricotta cheese, milk, melted butter, and salt to the spaghetti in the baking dish, and toss all until combined.

3. In a large nonstick skillet over medium-high heat, sauté olive oil, onion, and green bell pepper until peppers are crisp-tender, about 4 minutes.

4. Add marinara sauce and Parmesan cheese to the skillet and stir all to combine. Pour over spaghetti mixture in baking dish.

Shopping List

16 ounces **thin spaghetti**
1 tub (**15-16** ounces) **ricotta cheese**
¼ cup **milk**
3 tablespoons **butter** or **margarine**, melted
¼ teaspoon **salt**
1 tablespoon **olive oil**
1 small **yellow onion**, diced
⅓ cup diced **green bell pepper**
1 jar (**24-26** ounces) **marinara sauce**
⅓ cup **Parmesan cheese**
2 cups shredded **mozzarella cheese**
¼ teaspoon **Italian seasoning**

5. Top with mozzarella cheese and then sprinkle with the Italian seasoning. Cover with aluminum foil and bake 25 minutes. Remove foil and bake an additional 15-20 minutes, or until cheese begins to brown and sauce is bubbly. Let cool 5 minutes before serving.

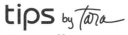
tips by Tara

For a full meal, simply add 1 pound of ground beef to the skillet in step 3, browning well before adding the onion and green bell pepper.

Whole Wheat Penne Primavera with Feta

Primavera means spring in Italian, and this quick meatless dish really earns its name because of all the colorful cut-up vegetables you can use to make it. Whole wheat penne keeps things light, while a combination of tangy feta and nutty Parmesan cheese complements the vegetables. Small and sweet grape tomatoes are in season year round and add a real fresh flavor.

1. Bring a large pot of salted water to a boil and cook penne according to package directions. Drain, reserving ½ cup of the pasta cooking water.

2. While pasta is cooking, heat olive oil and garlic in a large skillet over medium heat until the garlic is fragrant, about 2 minutes. Add the mixed vegetables and cherry tomatoes, and cook 4 minutes or until softened.

3. After draining pasta, transfer to a 3.5 quart temp-tations® baking dish. Cover with the cooked vegetables from the skillet and add feta and Parmesan cheeses, salt, pepper, and the reserved ½ cup of pasta cooking water. Toss all to combine and serve immediately.

Shopping List

1 box (**12-16** ounces) **whole wheat penne pasta**

2 tablespoons **olive oil**

2 teaspoons **minced garlic**

3 cups **frozen mixed vegetables**, rinsed to remove frost

1 cup **grape tomatoes**, halved

1 cup crumbled **feta cheese**

½ cup grated **Parmesan cheese**

½ teaspoon **salt**

¼ teaspoon **black pepper**

tips by *Tara*

If the pasta cools down too quickly, you can reheat by covering the dish in aluminum foil and baking in a 300 degree oven for 10 minutes, just until hot again.

pasta/rice

Baked Ziti Carbonara

Usually made with spaghetti in an eggy cream sauce, by legend, this dish originated with Italian charcoal makers who would slowly burn large pits of wood in the forests of Italy and make this simple dish with ingredients they could easily carry. It became popular after World War II when Italians feasted on eggs and bacon supplied by Americans.

1. Preheat oven to 350 degrees. Bring a large pot of salted water to a boil. Cook the ziti for 2 minutes less than the directions on the box, and then drain, reserving 1 cup of the pasta cooking water.

2. While the pasta is cooking, heat the olive oil in a large skillet over medium heat. Add the bacon and cook 3 minutes or until sizzling. Add the red pepper flakes and garlic, and cook 2 minutes more or until fragrant.

3. After draining the pasta, add the cream, eggs, parsley, black pepper, ½ cup of the Romano cheese, and the 1 cup of reserved pasta water to a 2.5 quart or larger temp-tations® baking dish. Add the pasta and toss together to combine.

4. Top casserole with the remaining Romano cheese and bake 15-20 minutes, or until bubbling hot. Serve immediately.

Shopping List

16 ounces **ziti pasta**

2 tablespoons **olive oil**

½ cup crumbled **pre-cooked bacon**

1 teaspoon **red pepper flakes**, optional

1 tablespoon **minced garlic**

½ cup **light cream** or **evaporated milk**

4 large **eggs**

¼ cup chopped **parsley**

¼ teaspoon **black pepper**

¾ cup grated **Romano cheese**

pasta/rice

tips by Tara

Use plenty of freshly ground black pepper here to make the flavor sparkle. The sharp, pungent flavor of Romano cheese, which originates in Rome, is perfect here but Parmesan or Asiago are good substitutes. The pasta water contains starch so it helps to thicken the sauce and make it creamy.

132 | shown in temp-tations® Vineyard 2.5 quart rectangular baker

temp-tations
presentable ovenware
by Tara

Creamy Rice and Succotash Casserole

This side dish casserole of mixed vegetables and rice in a (very!) creamy sauce is almost an entire meal in itself. Simply top or serve along with any meat dish, even simple baked or grilled chicken, and your dinner is set!

1. Preheat oven to 375 degrees. Place butter, yellow onion, and red bell pepper in a large nonstick skillet over medium-high heat, cooking for 4-5 minutes, just until the onions begin to turn translucent.

2. Add the condensed broccoli cheese soup, condensed cream of chicken soup, milk, and bay leaves (tear each slightly to help release their flavor, but keep them intact to easily remove) to the skillet, stirring constantly until everything is combined into a smooth sauce. Bring up to a simmer and then remove from heat and let sit at least 5 minutes.

3. Place rice and frozen vegetables into a 2.5 quart temp-tations® baking dish and cover with the sauce from the skillet. Stir all to combine, removing the 2 bay leaves as you find them.

Shopping List

1 tablespoon **butter** or **margarine**

½ cup diced **yellow onion**

½ cup diced **red bell pepper**

1 can **condensed broccoli cheese soup**, regular or low fat

1 can **cream of chicken soup**, regular or low fat

1 cup **milk**

2 **bay leaves**

3 cups **cooked rice**

16 ounces **frozen succotash vegetable medley** (peas, corn, carrots, green beans, and lima beans)

½ cup grated **Parmesan cheese**

4. Top with the grated Parmesan cheese and bake for 20 minutes, just until bubbly hot. Let cool 5 minutes before serving.

tips by Tara

Make this even easier with 2 pouches of pre-cooked rice like Uncle Ben's Ready Rice, sold near the instant rice in the grocery store. As it is already 100% cooked, you can add it straight into the casserole in step 3.

pasta/rice

Creamy Bow-tie Pasta with Mushrooms

Bow-tie pasta, also known as farfalle (which was derived from the Italian word for butterfly, not bow-tie), is the perfect shape for a dish like this one. All of the little ruffled ridges in the shape capture the creamy mushroom sauce well… not to mention, they're just something different than the usual spaghetti or penne!

1. Preheat oven to 350 degrees. Boil bow-tie pasta for 2 less minutes than the package directions. Drain and rinse under cold water. Transfer to a 3 quart temp-tations® baking dish.

2. In a large nonstick skillet over medium-high heat, heat butter until sizzling. Add mushrooms and cook 6-8 minutes, stirring only occasionally, until mushrooms begin to brown.

3. Reduce heat to medium and add condensed soups, milk, Parmesan cheese, and garlic powder, stirring until everything is combined. Remove from heat and stir in parsley flakes and Italian seasoning.

Shopping List

12 ounces **bow-tie (farfalle) pasta**

2 tablespoons **butter** or **margarine**

8 ounces sliced **mushrooms**

1 can **condensed cream of mushroom soup**

1 can **condensed cream of celery soup**

1 ½ cups **milk**

½ cup **Parmesan cheese**

¼ teaspoon **garlic powder**

1 tablespoon **parsley flakes**

½ teaspoon **Italian seasoning**

4. Pour the mushroom sauce over the bow tie pasta in the baking dish and toss all to coat.

5. Cover with aluminum foil and bake 20 minutes, until everything is hot and bubbly. Let cool 5 minutes before serving.

tips by Tara

For something really good, try topping with 1 cup of shredded, smoked Gouda cheese. Gouda cheese usually only comes in wedges, so you will have to shred it yourself, but it is worth it!

pasta/rice

Tara's Baked Manicotti

Manicotti comes from the Italian word for sleeve, because of their ridged open tube shape. For Italian families, it's a favorite dish for Sunday dinner because it's filling and delicious! Though it takes a little while to stuff each piece with the decadent cheese filling, this Italian specialty served in a tomato and Italian sausage sauce is well worth the effort!

1. Boil manicotti according to the package directions, undercooking by 2 minutes to keep them firm after baking. Drain and rinse under cold tap water.

2. Heat the olive oil in a large nonstick skillet over medium-high heat. Add the sausage and mushrooms, and brown 5 minutes, breaking up the sausage as it cooks. Lower heat to medium and add the remaining *Sauce* ingredients, simmering for 10 minutes.

3. In a mixing bowl, combine all *Filling* ingredients except ½ cup of the mozzarella cheese, and mix well. Place the filling in a large food storage bag and cut a one-inch slice from a bottom corner of the bag. Squeeze the bag in order to add a portion of the filling into each cooked manicotti. Repeat until all are stuffed.

4. Preheat the oven to 375 degrees. Pour ½ of the sauce into the bottom of a 4 quart temp-tations® baking dish. Arrange the manicotti in rows, and pour the remaining sauce over top. Sprinkle with the remaining ½ cup of mozzarella cheese and bake 30 minutes, or until the sauce is bubbling hot and cheese is browned. Let cool 5 minutes before serving.

Shopping List

1 (8 ounce) box **manicotti pasta**

SAUCE

2 tablespoons **olive oil**

½ pound **mild Italian sausage**, removed from casing

8 ounces sliced **mushrooms**

3 cups **tomato sauce**

1 teaspoon **oregano**

½ teaspoon **garlic powder**

FILLING

1 (15 ounce) container **part skim ricotta cheese**

2 cups shredded **mozzarella cheese**

¾ cup **Parmesan cheese**

10 ounces **frozen chopped spinach**, defrosted and water squeezed out

2 **eggs**

½ teaspoon **salt**

¼ teaspoon **black pepper**

tips by Tara

You may have enough pasta and filling to make a second layer of manicotti atop the first. If you do, be sure to spoon a thin layer of the sauce in between.

Prep Time   **Cook Time**   **Serves**   **3.5**

10   **27**   **6**   *Quart*

mins   mins

temp-tations
presentable ovenware
by Tara

Crispy Baked Gnocchi

Gnocchi are little Italian potato dumplings that are usually boiled and served soft, but I think that serving them this way is even better! After boiling, you coat them in a thin layer of Parmesan cheese and bake until they get super crispy, almost like little potato wedges, only soft and doughy on the inside! Serve as a side alongside anything you would ordinarily serve with potatoes or pasta. You can usually find dry gnocchi in the pasta aisle of the supermarket.

1. Preheat oven to 425 degrees. Drizzle the olive oil into the bottom of a 3.5 quart or larger temp-tations® rectangular baking dish.

2. In a large pot, boil gnocchi just until they float, 3-4 minutes. Drain and transfer to the greased baking dish. Toss to coat in the olive oil.

Shopping List

2 tablespoons **olive oil**

1 package (**15-18** ounces) **dry gnocchi**

¼ teaspoon **garlic powder**

⅛ teaspoon **salt**

⅛ teaspoon **pepper**

⅓ cup grated **Parmesan cheese**

3. Evenly sprinkle garlic powder, salt, and pepper over the gnocchi, and then cover with the Parmesan cheese. Toss again to coat on all sides.

4. Spread the gnocchi into a single layer at the bottom of the baking dish and bake 15 minutes.

5. Use a metal spatula to flip all gnocchi (they may seem stuck at first, but they will come up cleanly with a metal spatula). Return to the oven and bake an additional 8 minutes, until a light golden brown on both sides. Let cool in baking dish at least 5 minutes (these are HOT!). They will crisp up further as they cool.

tips by Tara

These also make a great appetizer for parties. As they bake in a single layer at the bottom of a large baking dish, I would suggest piling high in a smaller temp-tations® mixing bowl or baking dish after baking to serve.

pasta/rice

138 | shown in temp-tations® Old World 1.5 quart rectangular baker

Prep Time	Cook Time		Serves	1.5
10 *mins*	**30** *mins*		**4**	*Quart*

temp-tations
presentable ovenware
by Tara

Brown Rice Pilaf

I am not a very big fan of instant rice, especially instant brown rice, but non-instant whole grain brown rice like that used in this recipe takes an hour on the stove! Thankfully, that time is cut down immensely by microwaving right in a temp-tations® baking dish.

1. Place butter, yellow onion, mushrooms, and garlic in a 1.5 quart temp-tations® baking dish and microwave on high for 1 minute.

2. Add rice, chicken broth, water, poultry seasoning, and slivered almonds and stir until combined. Cover with plastic wrap, use a fork to pierce top of wrap in center, and microwave on high for 15 minutes.

3. Carefully remove wrap (dish will be very hot!) and stir. Return to microwave uncovered and heat on high an additional 10 minutes.

4. Stir one final time. Return to microwave and heat on high 5 final minutes.

Shopping List

1 tablespoon **butter** or **margarine**

½ cup diced **yellow onion**

½ cup diced **button** or **baby bella mushrooms**

2 teaspoons **minced garlic**

1 cup **whole grain brown rice**

2 cups **low sodium chicken broth**

1 ¼ cups **water**

¼ teaspoon **poultry seasoning**

¼ cup **slivered almonds**

salt and **pepper** to taste

pasta/rice

5. Let stand for 5 minutes, salt and pepper to taste, and fluff with a fork before serving garnished with fresh parsley, if desired.

tips *by Tara*

Stir in ⅓ cup of dried cranberries after removing from the microwave to turn this into a great Holiday Brown Rice Stuffing. Though it may seem underdone if you are not familiar, whole grain brown rice is chewier than white rice, which I believe works well as a pilaf.

Baked Ravioli with Broccoli and Black Olives

This baked dinner is one of the easiest meals you can throw together. Starting with frozen ravioli and broccoli, there is no need to thaw... simply place it all in the baking dish and forget about it! An hour later you have tender, cheese filled ravioli in red sauce with a good amount of healthy broccoli florets. All of these flavors bake together in the oven for a truly delicious result.

1. Preheat oven to 350 degrees.

2. Place all ingredients, except shredded cheese and Italian seasoning, in a 3 quart temp-tations® baking dish and toss to combine. (A 3 quart dish looks best, but a 3.5 quart dish has more room to mix.)

3. Top all with shredded Italian cheese blend. Sprinkle Italian seasoning over cheese.

4. Cover with aluminum foil and bake 40 minutes. Remove foil and bake an additional 20-25 minutes, or until cheese is browning and the sauce is hot and bubbly. Let cool 5 minutes before serving.

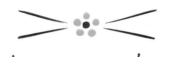

Shopping List

1 bag (**25** ounces) **frozen cheese ravioli**

10-12 ounces **frozen broccoli florets**

1 jar (**24-28** ounces) **marinara sauce**

3 tablespoons finely diced **yellow bell pepper**, optional

1 can (**2** ounces) **sliced black olives**, drained

⅓ cup grated **Parmesan cheese**

2 cups shredded **Italian cheese blend**

1 pinch **Italian seasoning**

tips by *Tara*

You can also purchase and make this with frozen meat filled ravioli for a more substantial dinner. You can also add ½ pound of ground beef browned in a skillet to the baking dish in step 2 for ravioli in meat sauce. Prepare in a 3.5 quart baking dish.

pasta/rice

Prep Time
25 mins

Cook Time
20 mins

Serves
6

2.5 Quart

temp-tations
presentable ovenware
by Tara

White Cheddar Mac and Cheese

A brick of really sharp Vermont white Cheddar cheese is a thing of beauty, and nobody ever said macaroni and cheese had to be yellow. So here's a little secret: you can serve a white version of mac and cheese like this one at even the nicest get togethers and your guests will feel like they're eating something refined, not off the kiddie menu!

1. Preheat oven to 375 degrees. Add butter and flour to a sauce pot over medium-high heat, stirring until a simmering paste is obtained. Simmer, stirring constantly for 4-5 minutes, until the paste turns slightly more golden in color.

2. Add Dijon mustard, milk, and salt, and whisk constantly, until combined and simmering. Once simmering, lower the heat to medium-low. Whisk in ⅔ of the white Cheddar cheese and all of the cream cheese a little at a time until combined. Remove from heat.

3. Add cooked pasta to a 2.5 quart temp-tations® baking dish and cover with the finished cheese sauce. Top the casserole with the remaining ⅓ of the white Cheddar cheese, and then sprinkle Italian breadcrumbs over top all.

4. Bake uncovered 15-20 minutes until cheese is bubbling and beginning to brown. Let cool 5 minutes before serving.

Shopping List

3 tablespoons **butter**

3 tablespoons **all purpose flour**

1 teaspoon **Dijon mustard**

3 cups **milk**

1 teaspoon **salt**

8 ounces **extra sharp white Cheddar cheese**, shredded

4 ounces **cream cheese**, regular or low fat

12 ounces **elbow macaroni**, undercooked by **2** minutes and drained

⅓ cup **Italian breadcrumbs**

tips by Tara

Substitute crumbled tortilla chips for the breadcrumbs, add ½ cup of frozen corn kernels and a package of pre-cooked southwestern seasoned chicken breast strips (sold near the lunch meats) for a complete Southwestern Mac and Cheese dinner!

pasta/rice

Side Dishes

144 | shown in temp-tations® Old World 2 quart square baker

Prep Time

5
mins

Cook Time

14
mins

Serves

4-6

2
Quart

temp-tations
presentable ovenware
by Tara

Green Beans with Cherries and Candied Pecans

This is my favorite way to prepare green beans, with tangy dried cherries and crunchy, candied pecans. The whole dish is made in only minutes, as you can candy the pecans on the stove as the green beans are heating in the microwave. I'm warning you now… you may want to make a double or triple batch of the pecans for dessert!

1. Place ¼ cup of tap water into a 2 quart temp-tations® baking dish.

2. Add green beans, butter, minced garlic, salt, and pepper to the water in the baking dish. Stir all, cover with plastic wrap, and use a fork to pierce a hole in the center of wrap. Microwave on high 7 minutes.

3. Make the candied pecans by combining butter, pecans, brown sugar, and cinnamon in a nonstick skillet over medium-high heat. Stir constantly just until brown sugar has melted and pecans are evenly coated, about 5 minutes. Remove from heat.

4. Carefully remove green bean dish from microwave, peel back plastic wrap, and then stir in dried cherries. Re-cover and microwave an additional 2 minutes, or until green beans are heated throughout.

5. Stir in candied pecans just before serving.

Shopping List

GREEN BEANS

1 large bag (**24** ounces) **frozen whole green beans**

2 tablespoons **butter** or **margarine**

1 rounded teaspoon **minced garlic**

¼ teaspoon **salt**

⅛ teaspoon **pepper**

⅓ cup **dried cherries**

CANDIED PECANS

1 tablespoon **butter** or **margarine**

⅔ cup **pecan halves**

2 tablespoons **light brown sugar**

⅛ teaspoon **ground cinnamon**

tips by Tara

Dried cherries aren't always available year round, but this is easily made with dried cranberries, like Craisins, in their place. You can also skip candying the pecans and simply stir them in plain if you are short on time or watching your sugar intake.

sides

Prep Time — 15 mins
Cook Time — 25 mins
Serves — 8
2 Quart

temp-tations®
presentable ovenware
by Tara

Broccoli & Cheddar Mashed Potato Bake

This dish can stand on its own as a lunch or accompany a dinner entrée for a heartier meal. It's quick and easy to make for those nights when friends drop over or when you just feel like something simple and delicious. Though it starts with instant mashed potatoes, the addition of broccoli, Cheddar cheese, and other ingredients ensures that you won't even be able to tell.

1. Preheat oven to 400 degrees. Prepare instant mashed potatoes according to package directions, and place in a 2 quart temp-tations® baking dish.

2. In a large skillet, sauté butter, onion, and garlic for 3 minutes, or until softened.

3. Add broccoli and cook 2 minutes longer or until crisp tender.

4. Pour broccoli mixture over mashed potatoes in baking dish and add milk, Parmesan cheese, salt, and pepper. Stir all until combined, smooth, and creamy.

5. Top with Cheddar cheese and bake 20-25 minutes or until the cheese is lightly browned. Serve hot.

Shopping List

4 cups prepared **instant mashed potatoes**
2 tablespoons **butter** or **margarine**
½ cup chopped **yellow onion**
1 teaspoon **minced garlic**
2 ½ cups chopped **broccoli**, thawed if frozen
½ cup **milk**
¼ cup grated **Parmesan cheese**
½ teaspoon **salt**
¼ teaspoon **black pepper**
1 cup shredded **Cheddar cheese**

tips by Tara

Making this with 4 cups of fresh mashed potatoes is even better, but obviously time consuming. This recipe is easy to make and can be made hours in advance or even a day ahead of time and then chilled. Simply allow 15 additional minutes in the oven if starting from a chilled state.

sides

Lemon Zucchini and Tomato Parmesan Casserole

Lemon pepper is an all-around great spice to keep in your pantry. It's made from the zest of the lemon, which is where the entire aroma comes from, and adds a bright, fresh flavor to this dish. This is an easy and colorful dish that is quickly prepared using fresh vegetables.

1. Preheat oven to 350 degrees. Spray a 1.5 quart temp-tations® baking dish with nonstick cooking spray.

2. In a large skillet over medium-high to high heat, sauté zucchini in 1 tablespoon of the olive oil until crisp-tender, about 3 minutes.

3. Add tomatoes to zucchini and pour into the greased baking dish.

4. In a mixing bowl, combine sour cream, eggs, salt, lemon pepper, and ⅔ of the Parmesan cheese, and then pour over the zucchini mixture in baking dish, stirring to combine.

Shopping List

nonstick cooking spray
4 cups sliced **zucchini**
2 tablespoons **olive oil**
2 cups sliced **plum** or **round tomatoes**
½ cup **sour cream**, regular or reduced fat
2 large **eggs**, beaten
½ teaspoon **salt**
2 teaspoons **lemon pepper**
½ cup grated **Parmesan cheese**
¼ cup **Italian breadcrumbs**

5. In a small bowl, combine breadcrumbs, remaining tablespoon of olive oil, and remaining Parmesan cheese and then evenly sprinkle over casserole.

6. Bake 40 minutes or until the topping is golden brown. Let cool 5 minutes before serving.

tips by Tara

I sometimes use yellow squash instead of, or in place of, ½ of the zucchini. This goes especially well with seafood or roast chicken.

sides

Prep Time | Cook Time | Serves | 2

10
mins

25
mins

9

Quart

temp-tations
presentable ovenware
by Tara

Cheddar Biscuit Bread

Making homemade biscuits can be a lot of work, but this recipe for a cheesy biscuit–like bread is one of the easiest breads you can make. Use a 2 quart temp-tations® square baking dish for best results, as this is prepared a whole lot like cornbread and cut into squares for serving. Who says a biscuit has to be round anyway?

1. Preheat oven to 425 degrees. Spray a 2 quart temp-tations® baking dish with nonstick cooking spray.

2. In a large mixing bowl, combine flour, baking powder, baking soda, and salt.

3. Mash or "cut" butter into the flour mixture until a thick and lumpy dough is beginning to form. (This is easiest with your hands.)

4. Add Cheddar cheese and buttermilk to the dough and stir until all are combined. (Dough will still be lumpy.)

Shopping List

nonstick cooking spray

2 cups **all purpose flour**

2 teaspoons **baking powder**

½ teaspoon **baking soda**

¾ teaspoon **salt**

6 tablespoons **butter** or **margarine**, softened

1 cup shredded **sharp Cheddar cheese**

1 ⅓ cups **buttermilk**

½ teaspoon **onion powder**

¼ teaspoon **paprika**

5. Spread dough into the greased baking dish, and then sprinkle the onion powder and paprika over top. Bake 20-25 minutes, or until bread is golden brown and set in the center. Let cool 5 minutes before cutting into 9 squares and serving hot.

tips by *Tara*

For a little heat, substitute cayenne pepper in place of the paprika in step 5. If serving alongside seafood, I like to sprinkle a large pinch of Old Bay seasoning over the top in place of the onion powder.

sides

Prep Time
15 mins

Cook Time
45 mins

Serves
6

3.5 Quart

temp-tations
presentable ovenware
by Tara

Rosemary Roasted Potatoes, Peppers, and Onions

Here I combine potatoes and sweet roasted veggies in one delicious and colorful dish! I often use naturally buttery-tasting gold potatoes because their skins, which contain most of the potato's nutrients and fiber, are usually thin enough that they don't require peeling. Large red potatoes are waxier and firmer, but also work well here.

1. Preheat oven to 400 degrees. Spray a 3.5 quart temp-tations® baking dish with nonstick cooking spray.

2. Place all of the ingredients in the greased baking dish, mixing well to combine.

3. Bake 45 minutes, stirring halfway through, or until the potatoes are crusty and tender.

Shopping List

nonstick cooking spray

2 pounds **gold or red potatoes**, quartered

1 **red bell pepper**, cut in thin strips

1 **green bell pepper**, cut in thin strips

1 medium **red onion**, sliced

4 teaspoons **minced garlic**

¼ cup **olive oil**

1 tablespoon chopped **fresh rosemary** or **1** teaspoon **dried rosemary**

1 teaspoon **salt**

¼ teaspoon **black pepper**

sides

tips by Tara

Fresh rosemary sprigs are the perfect garnish here. If you're using dried rosemary, be sure to crush it well because the whole leaves are sharp. A spice mill or mortar and pestle work well for this task.

Prep Time   Cook Time   Serves   2

5   9   6   Quart
mins   mins

temp-tations
presentable ovenware
by Tara

Green Beans Almondine

Green Beans Almondine is a classic and simple way to prepare green beans that the whole family will love. I make my version with frozen green beans, slivered almonds, and a few seasonings everyone will most likely already have in their cupboard. Microwaving right in a temp-tations® dish frees up your oven for cooking the main course.

1. Place ¼ cup of tap water into a 2 quart temp-tations® baking dish.

2. Add green beans, butter, garlic powder, onion powder, salt, and pepper to the water in the baking dish. Stir all, cover with plastic wrap, and use a fork to pierce a hole in the center of wrap. Microwave on high 7-9 minutes, or until green beans are steaming hot.

Shopping List

1 large bag (**20** ounces) **frozen whole green beans**

3 tablespoons **butter** or **margarine**

¼ teaspoon **garlic powder**

¼ teaspoon **onion powder**

¼ teaspoon **salt**

⅛ teaspoon **pepper**

½ cup **slivered almonds**

3. While green beans are cooking, toast the slivered almonds by placing in a dry skillet over medium heat. Shake the pan occasionally to keep them moving until almonds turn more golden in color, about 5 minutes.

4. Carefully remove green bean dish from microwave, unwrap, and then stir in toasted almonds. Serve hot.

tips by *Tara*

Sliced almonds can also be used in place of the slivered, but the sliced will toast very quickly in the skillet as they are so thin, so keep a close eye on them!

sides

Creamed Corn

This microwaveable creamed corn recipe won't have you husking any ears of corn, but is still a lot fresher tasting than the canned stuff. The secret ingredient is just a tiny dash of vanilla extract, which goes extremely well with the sweet corn.

1. Place butter and frozen corn kernels in a 2 quart temp-tations® baking dish, and microwave on high for 4 minutes, stirring halfway through.

2. Stir well, and then remove and transfer ½ cup of the corn kernels to the bowl of a food processor. Pulse the ½ cup of kernels until entirely pureed and then return to the baking dish.

3. Add the sugar, vanilla extract, salt, and 1 cup of the milk to the dish and stir all to combine. Top with the cream cheese and microwave on high for 8 minutes, stirring twice, until the cream cheese is entirely combined and everything is bubbly hot.

4. Whisk cornstarch into the remaining ¼ cup of milk, and then stir into the creamed corn. Return to the microwave and cook on high for a final 3 minutes. Stir well. Garnish with finely diced red bell pepper to add a little color, if desired.

Shopping List

3 tablespoons **butter** or **margarine**

32 ounces **frozen corn kernels**

1 ¼ cups **milk**

1 tablespoon **sugar**

¼ teaspoon **vanilla extract**

½ teaspoon **salt**

8 ounces **cream cheese**, regular or reduced fat

1 ½ tablespoons **cornstarch**

tips by Tara

I prefer a little bit of the corn blended into the sauce for the subtle golden color it adds, but pureeing ½ cup of corn in step 2 is not necessary, and the final dish will still be plenty creamy if you skip it. If the sauce tastes a little bit chalky, cook an additional 3 minutes, making sure that you can see the sauce visibly puffing up in the microwave, as this is when the starchiness of the cornstarch will cook out.

Prep Time
15
mins

Cook Time
40
mins

Serves
12

3.5
Quart

temp-tations
presentable ovenware
by Tara

Cranberry Sweet Potato Casserole

This casserole is so sweet and good that you could eat it as a dessert if you wanted to. A nice dish when expecting company, it can easily be prepared a day ahead, refrigerated, and baked just before serving. With Craisins and orange baked in and a doughy, pecan filled topping, it is definitely not your usual sweet potato casserole.

1. Preheat oven to 400 degrees.

2. In large mixing bowl, combine the *Filling* ingredients and pour into a 3.5 quart temp-tations® baking dish.

3. In a small mixing bowl, combine the *Topping* ingredients and spoon over filling.

4. Bake 40 minutes or until the filling is bubbling and the topping has browned. Cool 10 minutes before serving.

Shopping List

FILLING
3 pounds **sweet potatoes**, peeled and chopped
1 cup **dried cranberries** (Craisins)
½ cup **light brown sugar**
4 tablespoons **butter** or **margarine**, melted
grated **zest and juice of 1 orange**
1 teaspoon **cinnamon**
½ teaspoon **ground allspice**
½ teaspoon **salt**

TOPPING
½ cup **light brown sugar**
1 cup **all purpose flour**
1 cup **chopped pecans**
½ cup **butter** or **margarine**, melted

tips by Tara

You can also use fresh or frozen cranberries in place of the dried. Simply use 1 cup of fresh or frozen and increase the sugar in the filling to 1 full cup.

sides

Prep Time
10 mins

Cook Time
20 mins

Serves
6

2.5
Quart

temp-tations
presentable ovenware
by Tara

Cauliflower Polonaise

Cauliflower Polonaise is a French dish by way of Poland. With hard boiled eggs and crunchy toasted croutons, this is good enough to convert even the most die-hard cauliflower critic! Thrown together in only minutes, this is one of those recipes that is greater than the sum of its parts.

1. Preheat oven to 350 degrees. In a medium pot, steam or boil the cauliflower florets until crisp-tender, about 6 minutes. Drain well because any clinging water will make for soggy crouton crumbs in the final dish.

2. In a small pan over low heat, melt the butter and then add the croutons. Stir until the croutons are golden brown and crunchy, about 4 minutes, being careful not to let the crumbs get too dark.

Shopping List

1 small head **cauliflower,** broken into small florets

3 tablespoons **butter** or **margarine**

¾ cup crushed **croutons**

2 **hard-boiled eggs,** chopped

¼ cup chopped **parsley**

½ teaspoon **salt**

¼ teaspoon **black pepper**

2 tablespoons **Parmesan cheese**

1 **lemon** cut into **6** wedges

3. Combine the drained cauliflower, eggs, parsley, salt, pepper, and browned croutons in a 2.5 quart temp-tations® baking dish. Mix well.

4. Sprinkle with Parmesan cheese and bake just 5-10 minutes or until everything is nice and hot. Serve with lemon wedges to squeeze over top.

tips by Tara

Baking the final dish is not entirely necessary if you prepare the cauliflower and breadcrumbs at the same time, combining them while the cauliflower is still very hot.

sides

Prep Time

5
mins

Cook Time

16
mins

Serves

4

2
Quart

temp-tations
presentable ovenware
by Tara

Apricot Glazed Carrots

This simple side dish is easily made in the microwave, freeing up your stove and oven to make the rest of your meal (something that really comes in handy around the holidays). Using baby carrots instead of the traditional discs saves a ton of time you would ordinarily spend peeling and cutting whole carrots!

1. Place ¼ cup of tap water into a 1.5 quart temp-tations® baking dish.

2. Add carrots, butter, and light brown sugar to baking dish, stir, and cover with plastic wrap. Use a fork to pierce a hole in plastic wrap before microwaving on high for 10 minutes, stirring halfway through.

3. Carefully remove dish from microwave, discard plastic wrap, and then stir in apricot preserves, salt, and nutmeg.

Shopping List

1 large bag (32 ounces) **baby carrots**

3 tablespoons **butter** or **margarine**

1 tablespoon **light brown sugar**

⅓ cup **apricot preserves**

¼ teaspoon **salt**

⅛ teaspoon **ground nutmeg**

2 teaspoons **cornstarch**

4. Microwave uncovered on high for an additional 2 minutes. Stir in cornstarch until completely dissolved, and microwave for 3-4 minutes, until carrots are tender and sauce is thickened. Use a slotted spoon to drain any excess liquid as you serve.

tips by Tara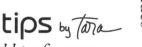

Orange marmalade also works well in place of the apricot preserves. If you would prefer your carrots less sweet, the brown sugar can be left out entirely.

sides

Smoky BBQ Baked Beans

This smoky, sweet baked bean casserole is a perfect accompaniment to hot dogs, hamburgers, and other picnic fare like deli-style sandwiches. Double the recipe for an easy crowd-pleasing dish for a pot-luck dinner or buffet. I like to use white beans, sometimes called cannellini, because of their thin skins and velvety texture, but great northern or pinto beans are good substitutes as well.

1. Preheat oven to 350 degrees.

2. In a 2.5 quart temp-tations® baking dish, combine all ingredients except brown sugar, mixing well.

3. Sprinkle brown sugar over top all, cover with aluminum foil, and bake 1 ½ hours.

4. Uncover and continue baking an additional 30 minutes or until top is browned. Cool 10 minutes before serving.

Shopping List

2 (**16** ounce) cans **white beans**, drained and rinsed

½ cup crumbled **pre-cooked bacon**

½ pound **kielbasa sausage**, diced

½ cup chopped **yellow onion**

½ cup chopped **green bell pepper**

2 teaspoons **minced garlic**

1 cup **barbecue sauce**

1 tablespoon **yellow mustard**

1 tablespoon **Worcestershire sauce**

1 teaspoon **hot sauce**, optional

¼ cup **dark brown sugar**

sides

tips by Tara

Kielbasa is a mild, smoky Polish style sausage which adds another layer of smoky flavor to these juicy, saucy beans. You can also try substituting Mexican chorizo sausage, which is also smoky, only much, much spicier.

Lisa's Calico Beans

My mother's friend Lisa cooked for her church's after-school program (as did my mother). This was one of Lisa's signature after school dishes, where a little can go a long, long way. I'm not exactly sure the significance of adding a can of pork and beans to a big dish of homemade pork and beans, but I definitely know that this dish works!

1. Preheat oven to 375 degrees.

2. In a large skillet over medium-high heat, sauté chopped bacon until nearly crispy.

3. Add onions to skillet and sauté until bacon is crispy and onions are translucent. Drain well.

4. Transfer drained bacon and onions to a 2.5 quart temp-tations® baking dish and cover with remaining ingredients. Stir well to combine.

5. Bake 40-45 minutes, or until bubbly hot. Serve immediately.

Shopping List

1 pound **bacon**, chopped
1 large **onion**, chopped
1 can **pork and beans**
1 can **red kidney beans**, drained
1 can **white northern beans**, drained
1 can **butter beans**, drained
1 cup **ketchup**
½ cup **sugar**
½ cup **light brown sugar**
1 tablespoon **vinegar**

tips by Tara

1 pound of ground beef or pork sausage can be added in place of, or along with the bacon to make this into a hearty main course.

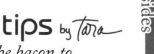

sides

| shown in temp-tations® Old World 1 quart pie plate

Prep Time

20
mins

Cook Time

55
mins

Serves

6

1
Quart

temp-tations
Presentable ovenware
by Tara

Spinach Pie

This recipe is a lot like a quiche that is dense with spinach, yet made creamy with the addition of ricotta cheese. Spinach pies are typically Greek and made in puffed pastry, but my recipe is more Italian and has a traditional pie crust that holds together better.

1. Preheat oven to 350 degrees. Unroll pie crust and place in a 1 quart temp-tations® pie plate. Fold down and press top of crust into fluted edges of the pie plate.

2. Place olive oil and yellow onion in a nonstick skillet over medium-high heat, cooking the onions until they turn translucent and begin to caramelize.

3. Add the chopped spinach to the onions in the pan and cook just until warmed throughout, about 5 minutes. Drain spinach and onions well.

4. In a large temp-tations® mixing bowl, whisk the eggs until frothy. Whisk in ricotta cheese, Parmesan cheese, Italian seasoning, salt, and pepper until well combined. Finally, fold in mozzarella cheese and the drained spinach and onions.

5. Pour the finished filling into the pie crust and bake for 50-55 minutes, or until crust is well browned and a toothpick inserted into the center of the pie comes out mostly clean. Let cool 10 minutes before slicing into 6 equal slices.

Shopping List

1 rolled **9** inch **pie crust**, room temperature

1 tablespoon **olive oil**

¾ cup diced **yellow onion**

10 ounces **frozen chopped spinach**

4 large **eggs**

1 cup **ricotta cheese**

⅓ cup grated **Parmesan cheese**

½ teaspoon **Italian seasoning**

½ teaspoon **salt**

¼ teaspoon **pepper**

1 ¼ cups shredded **mozzarella cheese**

tips by Tara

The pie crust used in this recipe is usually sold in a box of 2, near the cans of biscuits in the refrigerated case. The pie will puff up when cooking, but go down to a normal size as it cools.

sides

Prep Time
10 mins

Cook Time
30 mins

Serves
12

3.5 Quart

temp-tations
presentable ovenware
by Tara

Southern Honey Cornbread

Buttermilk makes this homemade Southern cornbread tender and fluffy. Fair warning: in the South they like their cornbread sweet! Even just a little bit of honey adds plenty of honey flavor, while also keeping the bread extra moist.

1. Preheat oven to 375 degrees. Spray a 3.5 quart temp-tations® baking dish with nonstick cooking spray.

2. In a large mixing bowl, add the sugar, honey, eggs, butter, and buttermilk, mixing just until combined.

3. In another mixing bowl, combine the cornmeal, flour, baking powder, and salt. While stirring, add the cornmeal mixture to the egg mixture, mixing only enough to combine. (The mixture will be a little lumpy.)

Shopping List

nonstick cooking spray

1 cup **sugar**

¼ cup **honey**

2 eggs, beaten

½ cup **butter** or **margarine**, melted

2 cups **buttermilk**

2 cups **yellow** or **white cornmeal**

2 cups **flour**

2 teaspoons **baking powder**

1 teaspoon **salt**

4. Pour into the greased baking dish and bake 30 minutes or until top is golden brown. Cut into 12 squares to serve.

sides

tips by Tara

This bread freezes perfectly. Simply defrost, wrap in foil, and bake in the oven for 15 minutes at 375 degrees. Serve alongside salty, savory dishes like country ham, pulled pork, or my Ranch Chicken Casserole, recipe page: 87.

Southern Vidalia Onion Potato Salad

This is my favorite potato salad and a great side dish, but an even better part of any party buffet. I particularly appreciate that the ingredients are always in my pantry. Personally, I like to assemble this salad fast, after boiling the potatoes so that their heat transfers to the other ingredients to serve this warm, but of course it's great chilled as well!

1. Bring a large pot of salted water to a boil and cook cut potatoes until tender but firm, about 12 minutes. Drain and transfer to a 2.5 quart or larger temp-tations® mixing bowl, or an oval or round baking dish.

2. Cover potatoes with remaining ingredients, except salt and paprika. Toss gently until all are combined.

3. Salt to taste and sprinkle with paprika before serving warm. If serving cold: after boiling potatoes, rinse under cold running water and continue recipe as written. Refrigerate for at least 1 hour before serving.

Shopping List

3 pounds **gold potatoes**, peeled if desired, cut into large chunks

½ cup diced **Vidalia onion**

½ cup diced **celery**

6 hard-boiled eggs, chopped

1 cup **mayonnaise**

¼ cup diced **pimento**

¼ cup **pickle relish**

2 tablespoons **yellow mustard**

2 tablespoons **sugar**

½ teaspoon **black pepper**

1 teaspoon **hot sauce**, optional

salt to taste

1 teaspoon **paprika**, for garnish

tips by Tara

Vidalia onions come from Vidalia, Georgia and are quite sweet and mild. If you substitute regular onions, soak them in a bowl of ice water for 15 minutes, then drain. This will magically get rid of that strong onion taste!

sides

Grandma Frances' Zucchini Casserole

This is my Grandma Frances' famous zucchini casserole! Just be sure you have a whole lot of mouths to feed whenever you prepare this delicious side dish, as this casserole is massive! Though chopping all of the vegetables may take some time, nowadays you can buy shoestring or matchstick carrots already cut in the grocery store to save a little time.

1. Preheat oven to 350 degrees.

2. In a 4 or 5 quart temp-tations® baking dish, combine zucchini, carrots, onions, cream of mushroom soup, cream of celery soup, and sour cream. Mix well.

3. Add ½ of the stuffing cubes until evenly distributed.

4. Top casserole with the remaining stuffing cubes, and then pour melted butter over top all. Cover with aluminum foil and bake for 30 minutes.

5. Remove aluminum foil and bake an additional 30 minutes, until casserole is bubbly and stuffing cubes are well browned. Let sit 5 minutes before serving.

Shopping List

6 medium **zucchini** (about **3** pounds), peeled and cubed

3 carrots, grated or shredded

2 onions, chopped

1 can (**10** ounces) **condensed cream of mushroom soup**

1 can (**10** ounces) **condensed cream of celery soup**

16 ounces **sour cream**, regular or reduced fat

1 large bag (**14** ounces) **stuffing cubes**

2 sticks **butter** or **margarine** (can use **1**), melted

tips by Tara

While this is my grandma's casserole, exactly as she makes it for holidays and family get togethers, it can easily be halved for smaller gatherings and made in a 2 or 2.5 quart temp-tations® baking dish. Using both cream of mushroom and cream of celery soups is not necessary, as you can make this with one or the other instead.

sides

Carrot and Raisin Salad

This carrot and raisin salad recipe is how my family has been making the barbecue staple for as long as I can remember. Letting the salad marinate for 2 hours in the refrigerator really brings out the sugars in the carrots, dressing, pineapple, and raisins... it's no wonder that even the pickiest kids find this salad irresistible.

1. Add all ingredients to a 1.5 quart temp-tations® mixing bowl or baking dish.

2. Toss all until fully combined, cover, and refrigerate for at least 2 hours before serving alongside picnic or barbecue fare.

Shopping List

3 cups shredded carrots

1 cup crushed pineapple, drained

½ cup **prepared salad dressing** (like Miracle Whip)

¾ cup **raisins**

¼ teaspoon **salt**

⅛ teaspoon **nutmeg**

tips by Tara

Store bought shredded or "matchstick" carrots work best in this salad. You can also make your own if you have the right attachment for your food processor, but check the carrot section of the produce aisle first, as they usually carry them pre-shredded now. You can also substitute shredded "broccoli slaw", sold in bags in the produce section, for a little more nutrition.

sides

Summer Squash Casserole

It's no secret that kids love macaroni and cheese, but I can tell you that kids love squash and cheese too… all it takes is one bite! Squash are quite resilient, so you can prepare this creamy casserole up to a day in advance and simply pop it in the oven whenever you're ready to bake.

1. Preheat oven to 375 degrees. Place butter in a 2.5 quart temp-tations® baking dish and microwave 10-20 seconds, just until melted. Shake dish from side to side to thoroughly coat bottom and sides.

2. In a large mixing bowl, combine all remaining ingredients, except cracker crumbs, tossing until mixed.

3. Pour the contents of the mixing bowl into the greased baking dish, cover with aluminum foil, and bake 25 minutes.

4. Remove foil, top with cracker crumbs, and continue baking an additional 15-20 minutes, or until squash is tender. Let rest 5-10 minutes before serving.

Shopping List

2 tablespoons **butter** or **margarine**

4 large **yellow squash**, sliced

¼ teaspoon **black pepper**

¼ teaspoon **garlic powder**

3 **green onions**, sliced

1 can (**10** ounces) **condensed Cheddar cheese soup**

¾ cup **milk**

1 cup shredded **sharp Cheddar cheese**

¾ cup **buttery cracker crumbs**

tips by Tara

Add chopped pimentos to the casserole in step 2 to add a little bit more color. If you like broccoli (who doesn't?), condensed broccoli and cheese soup can be substituted in place of the Cheddar soup for even more flavor.

sides

Prep Time   Cook Time   Serves   4

20   1.5   12   Quart
mins   hours

temp-tations
presentable ovenware
by Tara

White Bean and Kielbasa Cassoulet

Cassoulet comes from the countryside of Southwest France where the preparation varies greatly from town to town. Similar to American baked beans, the traditional cassoulet is slow-baked overnight. Unlike sweet American baked beans, the flavor of this dish is savory with herbs and plenty of garlic. Also, this is one of those wonderful dishes that tastes better reheated!

1. Preheat oven to 400 degrees. Heat 2 tablespoons olive oil in a large non-stick skillet over medium-high heat. Add carrots, onions, and garlic, and sauté five minutes or until softened.

2. Pour the sautéed vegetable mixture into a 4 quart temp-tations® baking dish, add the remaining *Cassoulet* ingredients, and mix well.

3. In a small bowl, combine breadcrumbs and olive oil, and sprinkle over top all in baking dish.

4. Bake 1 ½ hours, or until the beans are bubbling and the topping is browned and crispy. Serve hot.

Shopping List

CASSOULET

2 tablespoons **olive oil**

1 cup diced **carrots**

1 cup diced **yellow onion**

1 tablespoon **minced garlic**

3 (16 ounce) cans **cannellini beans**, drained and rinsed

1 cup **low sodium chicken broth**

1 cup **jarred marinara sauce**

1 pound **kielbasa sausage**, sliced

1 ½ teaspoons **Italian seasoning**

½ teaspoon **black pepper**

TOPPING

1 cup soft **breadcrumbs**

2 tablespoons **olive oil**

tips by Tara

One of the characteristics of a true cassoulet is the crust, so I like to make my own "soft" breadcrumbs in a food processor using plain Italian or French bread. You can substitute Panko breadcrumbs or your favorite dried breadcrumbs.

sides

Desserts

Prep Time	Cook Time		Serves	2
15 mins	**45** mins		**9**	*Quart*

temp-tations
presentable ovenware
by Tara

White Chocolate Macadamia Blondies

This is one of my all time favorite dessert recipes to make in a temp-tations® dish. Like an exact cross between a brownie and a white chocolate macadamia nut cookie, you'll be surprised at just how thick and chewy these turn out to be! What makes them even more decadent is that most of the white chocolate chips dissolve right into the dough as they bake, making these extra fudgy.

1. Preheat oven to 350 degrees and spray a 2 quart temp-tations® baking dish with nonstick cooking spray.

2. In a large bowl, whisk together melted butter, brown sugar, egg, and vanilla extract until well combined.

3. Using a rubber spatula, gently stir in flour and baking powder until a batter that is free of lumps is created.

4. Fold white chocolate morsels and macadamia nuts into the batter, and then scrape out of the bowl and into the greased baking dish.

5. Bake for 40-45 minutes, or until the top is golden brown and the center has risen well. Cool at least 1 hour on a wire rack before slicing into 9 squares to serve.

Shopping List

nonstick cooking spray

1 ½ sticks (¾ cup) **butter** or **margarine**, melted

1 ½ packed cups **light brown sugar**

1 large **egg**

2 teaspoons **vanilla extract**

1 ½ cups **all purpose flour**

1 ½ teaspoons **baking powder**

¾ cup **white chocolate morsels**

1 cup **macadamia nuts**

tips by Tara

Since these will most likely be very popular around your house, why not make a double batch in my 4 quart 13x9 temp-tations® baking dish?

desserts

Prep Time	Cook Time		Serves	1
25 mins	**55** minutes		**6**	**Quart**

temp-tations®
presentable ovenware
by Tara

Pecan Pie

Pecan pie seems difficult, but it is actually one of the easiest pies that you can make. With only a few ingredients and minimal effort, you can have a homemade piece of chewy, gooey, sweet, and delicious pie that will definitely leave you feeling accomplished… or at least surprised that it really was that easy!

1. Preheat oven to 350 degrees. Generously spray a 1 quart temp-tations® pie plate with nonstick cooking spray and then sprinkle with about 1 tablespoon of flour. Unroll pie crust and place in pie plate. Fold down and press top of crust into fluted edges of the pie plate. When folding crust, keep it at least as high as the pie plate and be extremely careful not to tear the crust, or the filling will leak and cause the crust to stick.

2. Sprinkle 2 tablespoons of flour along the bottom of the pie crust and refrigerate 10 minutes.

3. In a large mixing bowl, combine eggs with sugar, brown sugar, flour, and vanilla extract. Fold in corn syrup and butter, until everything is well combined.

Shopping List

nonstick cooking spray

all purpose flour, for the dish

1 rolled **9** inch **pie crust,** room temperature

3 eggs, very lightly beaten

2 tablespoons **sugar**

¾ cup **dark brown sugar**

1 ½ tablespoons **all purpose flour**

1 teaspoon **vanilla extract**

⅔ cup **corn syrup**

2 tablespoons **butter,** melted

1 rounded cup **pecan halves**

4. Place the pecan halves at the bottom of the pie crust and pour the filling over top. (Pecan halves will float to the top.)

5. Bake 50-55 minutes, or until pie is somewhat springy in the center (it will jiggle like gelatin, but will continue cooking once removed from the oven). Check on pie periodically as it cooks, and surround the edges of the crust with tin foil if they begin to over-brown. Cool completely before serving.

tips by Tara

Once the pecans have floated up to the top of the pie in step 3, use a fork or knife to flip them right side up to ensure the best looking pie.

desserts

temp-tations
presentable ovenware
by Tara

Tara's Over the Top S'more Brownies

This recipe is the best of both worlds—you get s'mores and you get brownies! With graham crackers at the bottom and marshmallows and chocolate chips baked in and on top, these brownies are like none you've ever had. It's no wonder the word "s'more" means "some more" as you'll definitely want more of these gooey, chewy treats!

1. Preheat oven to 350 degrees. Spray a 3.5 quart temp-tations® baking dish with nonstick cooking spray.

2. Completely cover the bottom of the baking dish with a single layer of graham crackers.

3. In a large mixing bowl, prepare brownie mix according to package directions. Add vanilla extract, 1 cup of the miniature marshmallows, and ½ cup of the chocolate chips to the batter, gently folding in.

Shopping List

nonstick cooking spray

6 double **graham crackers**

1 (17.6 oz package) **dark fudge brownie mix**

1 teaspoon **vanilla extract**

3 cups **miniature marshmallows**

1 ½ cups **semisweet chocolate chips**

4. Pour the batter over the graham crackers, using a spatula to spread evenly throughout dish. Bake 30 to 40 minutes until set and a toothpick inserted into the center comes out mostly clean.

5. Remove the pan from the oven and sprinkle the remaining marshmallows and chocolate chips over the top. Bake 5 additional minutes and then let cool for 5 more. Slice into 16 squares and serve warm.

tips by Tara

The longer you let them cool, the less messy they will be to cut and eat. Cutting once cooled will result in a cleaner look that can still reheat in the microwave to serve warm. Still, I say that s'mores should be messy!

desserts

Prep Time
15 mins

Cook Time
45 mins

Serves
12

2.5 Quart

temp-tations
presentable ovenware
by Tara

Blueberry Peach Cobbler

No longer just enjoyed in summer, this wonderful combination of fruit can be found in the freezer section all year round. Frozen fruit is usually sweeter and juicier than fresh because only the ripest fruit is selected.

1. Preheat oven to 400 degrees. In a large mixing bowl, combine all *Filling* ingredients and let sit 10 minutes for the instant tapioca to soften. Pour into a 2.5 quart temp-tations® baking dish.

2. In another large mixing bowl, combine Bisquick baking mix, cinnamon, and 2 tablespoons of the sugar. Pour in the cream and stir just long enough to make soft dough. (Over mixing will make it tough.)

3. Evenly drop by the spoonful over top of the fruit mixture, and then drizzle with the melted butter. Sprinkle remaining sugar over top all.

4. Bake 40-45 minutes on the bottom rack of the oven, or until the biscuit topping is golden and the fruit is bubbling. Serve warm, topped with vanilla ice cream.

Shopping List

FILLING

1 bag (**16 ounces**) **frozen peach slices**

1 bag (**16 ounces**) **frozen blueberries**

¾ cup **sugar**

2 tablespoons **instant tapioca**

2 tablespoons **flour**

TOPPING

2 ½ cups **Bisquick baking mix**

½ teaspoon **cinnamon**

¼ cup **sugar**

1 cup **light cream** or **evaporated milk**

2 tablespoons **butter** or **margarine**, melted

tips by Tara

1 tablespoon of corn starch can be used in place of the instant tapioca to thicken the cobbler, but tapioca will give better results. If using fresh fruit, bake on the oven rack second from the top and reduce baking time to 25–30 minutes, or until bubbly.

desserts

temp-tations
presentable ovenware
by Tara

Orange and Cream Gelatin Parfait

This parfait is a really light and refreshing dessert that you can easily prepare in advance to lighten your load come dinnertime. Cut into squares and serve from the temp-tations® baking dish into clear beverage or wine glasses for the best presentation!

1. Place 1 ½ cups of water in a 1.5 quart temp-tations® baking dish and microwave for 2 minutes, until boiling hot.

2. Add 1 box of the orange gelatin to the boiling water and stir for 2 minutes, until completely dissolved.

3. Drain the juice of the can of Mandarin oranges into the hot gelatin mixture, stirring to combine, and then drop the mandarin oranges into the gelatin evenly. Refrigerate for 1 hour, or until almost completely set.

Shopping List

2 boxes (**3 ounces each**) **orange flavored gelatin**, may use sugar free

1 can (**8-10 ounces**) **Mandarin oranges**

⅔ tub (**8 ounces**) **non-dairy whipped topping**, regular or light, thawed

fresh **orange zest**, optional

4. Prepare the second box of gelatin in a large temp-tations® mixing bowl by stirring into ¾ cup of boiling water for 2 minutes. Add ¾ of a cup of ice cold water and stir. Place in freezer for 15 minutes, just until very cool, but not set.

5. Place the non-dairy whipped topping into a blender and cover with the cooled gelatin from the mixing bowl. Pulse blender 4-5 times, just until smooth.

6. Pour this second, creamy mixture, over the mandarin orange gelatin in the refrigerator and refrigerate all for 2 hours or until well set. Serve sprinkled with fresh orange zest, if desired.

tips by Tara

You can make a Strawberries and Cream Parfait by replacing the orange gelatin with strawberry gelatin, the mandarin oranges with ¾ cup of sliced strawberries, and the mandarin orange juice with ½ cup of cold water or white grape juice.

desserts

Cinnamon Carnival Nuts

I've always loved the cinnamon and sugar glazed nuts you can purchase in a paper cone at carnivals or fairs, and this recipe does a very good job recreating their flavor at home, but with an even better—almost peanut brittle like—texture.

1. Preheat oven to 400 degrees. Combine butter and 1 cup of the sugar and spread into a 4-quart temp-tations® baking dish.

2. Bake 20 minutes or until the sugar melts and starts to brown. Stir once, then place back in the oven to bake 10 minutes longer or until evenly browned. Be careful when handling, this mixture is VERY hot!

3. Add the nuts along with 2 tablespoons of tap water and stir to combine.

Shopping List

6 tablespoons **butter** or **margarine**, melted

1 ¼ cups **sugar**

3 (**10** ounce) cans or **6** cups **roasted and salted mixed nuts**

2 teaspoons **cinnamon**

4. Bake 15 additional minutes, until the nuts are well coated in shiny, sugary syrup. Remove from oven and let cool 10 minutes.

5. In a large mixing bowl, combine the cinnamon with remaining ¼ cup sugar. Stir in nuts, tossing to coat evenly.

6. Spread onto waxed paper and cool to room temperature, about 15 minutes. Break apart, into bite-sized clumps. Serve on a temp-tations® platter or piled high in your favorite temp-tations® baking dish.

tips by Tara

The salt cuts the sweetness of the sugar coating and balances the spices, but you can certainly make this treat with unsalted nuts if you prefer. Adding ¼ teaspoon of cayenne pepper will add a tinge of heat to the sweet for something entirely new.

desserts

Prep Time
20
mins

Cook Time
65
mins

Serves
12

2.5
Quart

temp-tations
presentable ovenware
by Tara

Raspberry Cheesecake Bars

These raspberry cheesecake bars are not only easy and delicious; they're beautiful too! With just the right amount of raspberries swirled throughout to give them a little tartness, they're not as sweet and heavy as you would expect from cheesecake.

1. Preheat oven to 350 degrees and spray a 2.5 quart temp-tations® baking dish with nonstick cooking spray.

2. Mix *Crust* ingredients and press into the bottom of the baking dish until well compacted. Bake 15 minutes and then cool on wire rack for 15 minutes as you prepare the filling.

3. Place all *Filling* ingredients, except raspberries, in a large bowl and whisk together until very well combined. Use an electric mixer for best results. Pour filling over baked crust in baking dish.

4. In a blender or food processor, puree raspberries until almost entirely smooth. Spoon purée onto filling in baking dish and run a butter knife or spatula through all, swirling the purée throughout.

Shopping List

nonstick cooking spray

CRUST

1 ½ cups **graham cracker crumbs**

4 tablespoons **butter** or **margarine**, melted

3 tablespoons **sugar**

FILLING

3 packages (**8 ounces each**) **cream cheese**, softened

¾ cup **sugar**

2 large **eggs**

1 teaspoon **vanilla extract**

½ cup fresh **raspberries**

5. Bake in the 350 degree oven for about 45 minutes, until the center is somewhat springy and toothpick inserted into a white part of the cake comes out clean. Cool at least 30 minutes on a wire rack before refrigerating at least 3 hours. Slice into 12 bars to serve.

tips by Tara

For even more raspberry flavor, spread raspberry preserves over top of the chilled and sliced bars before serving!

desserts

| shown on temp-tations® Old World salad plate, with Old World loaf pan

Chocolate Chip Pound Cake

With an abundance of chocolate chips and sour cream to keep it extra moist, this pound cake is a simple and foolproof dessert that you can get in the oven in only minutes (it takes a little bit longer from there)! It's even better when you top it with the easy icing recipe in my tips below.

1. Preheat oven to 350 degrees. Spray a 1.7 quart temp-tations® loaf pan with nonstick cooking spray.

2. In a large bowl or electric mixer, whisk butter and sugar until well combined and fluffy. Beat in eggs and sour cream a little at a time.

3. Slowly fold vanilla extract, baking powder, and flour into the mixture to create a batter.

4. Pour batter into greased loaf pan and top with chocolate chips. Gently stir chocolate chips into the batter.

5. Cover with aluminum foil and bake for 1 hour and 15 minutes. Remove foil and continure baking for an additional 45 minutes, or until cake is set and a toothpick inserted into the center comes out mostly clean. Cool completely before serving.

Shopping List

nonstick cooking spray
2 sticks (**1 cup**) **butter**, softened
1 ½ cups **sugar**
4 eggs
½ cup **sour cream**
2 teaspoons **vanilla extract**
½ teaspoon **baking powder**
1 ¾ cups **all purpose flour**
¾ cup **milk chocolate chips**

tips by Tara

Make an icing to top the pound cake before it cools by combining 3 tablespoons of hot, melted butter or margarine, with 1 cup of powdered sugar. Pour over pound cake while still hot and let cool with the cake.

desserts

182 | shown in temp-tations® Old World set of 6 muffin cups with tray

temp-tations®
presentable ovenware
by Tara

Chocolate Covered Cherry Cookie Cups

This recipe may just be the single easiest and most impressive of all of my recipes! With only three simple ingredients, you can bake up a delicious and perfectly portioned dessert brimming with hot gooey chocolate and cherries, and topped with a crispy sugar cookie topping.

1. Preheat oven to 325 degrees. Arrange 6 temp-tations® individual 4 ounce muffin cups in front of you.

Shopping List

1 can (**21** ounces) **cherry pie filling**

6 rounded tablespoons **chocolate chips**

1 package (**16** ounces) **ready-to-bake sugar cookie dough** (the kind in the rectangular package, not the tube)

2. Place 2 rounded tablespoons of the cherry pie filling into each muffin cup.

3. Add 1 rounded tablespoon of chocolate chips over cherry pie filling in each cup.

4. Place 1 square of cookie dough in the center of each cup. Wrap and refrigerate remaining cookie dough and cherry pie filling to make a second batch of cups, or simply bake the remaining cookies when you desire.

5. Bake all 6 cups directly on the center oven rack for 25-28 minutes, or until filling is bubbling up and the cookie topping is golden brown. Let cool 10 minutes before serving as these are HOT.

tips by Tara

It may not seem full enough at first, but the filling will bubble up quite a lot in the oven, and adding any more cherry pie filling may result in it bubbling over.

desserts

Prep Time

20
mins

Cook Time

0
mins

Serves

8-10

1.5
Quart

temp-tations
presentable ovenware
by Tara

Honey Lime Fruit Salad

A good, light fruit salad makes a really great potluck dish, as most people tend to bring heavier hot dishes. To save on prep time, I like to use a combination of fresh fruits and refrigerated jarred fruits, usually found near the fresh produce. Still, using all fresh fruits in this recipe is always a welcome substitute.

1. Combine all *Salad* ingredients in a 1.5 quart temp-tations® baking dish.

2. In a mixing bowl, combine the yogurt, honey, lime juice, and lime zest.

3. Cover and refrigerate salad and dressing separately until ready to serve, up to 1 day. Just before serving, drizzle some of the dressing over salad and sprinkle with the almonds. Serve alongside a small dish of the remaining dressing for those who may want more.

Shopping List

SALAD

4 **kiwi**, peeled and chopped

1 jar (**24** ounces) refrigerated **mandarin oranges**, drained

1 jar (**24** ounces) refrigerated **mango slices**, drained and cut into smaller pieces

2 cups **seedless grapes**

1 can (**20** ounces) **pineapple chunks**, drained

DRESSING

1 cup **vanilla yogurt**

2 tablespoons **honey**

juice of **2 limes**

1 teaspoon grated **lime zest**

¼ cup **toasted sliced almonds**

tips by Tara

Fruit salad can be as varied as you like. Fresh sliced apples work well in place of the mango slices, just be sure to toss the salad in a small amount of dressing immediately after cutting the apples, as the lime juice will keep them from turning brown.

desserts

temp-tations
presentable ovenware
by Tara

Chocolate Bread Pudding

What could be better than bread pudding? How about chocolate bread pudding?! This dessert contains cinnamon and allspice, a combination of aromatic and sweet spices that's a favorite in Mexico. This recipe is great for using any leftover or reduced (day-old) bread.

1. Spray a 2 quart temp-tations® baking dish with nonstick cooking spray. Remove crusts from sliced bread and discard. Cut bread into small cubes, about 12 per slice. Place cubes in greased baking dish as you go.

2. In a sauce pot over medium-high heat, heat cream, stirring constantly, until simmering. Remove from heat and stir in chocolate chips, stirring until chocolate has completely melted.

3. In a large mixing bowl, beat the eggs and brown sugar until well mixed. Stir in the butter, cinnamon, and allspice, and then slowly add the hot chocolate mixture, whisking until all is combined.

Shopping List

nonstick cooking spray

8 ounces **Italian bread**, sliced

2 cups **light cream** or **evaporated milk**

2 cups **semi-sweet chocolate chips**

4 large **eggs**

1 cup **dark brown sugar**

6 tablespoons **butter** or **margarine**, melted

1 teaspoon **cinnamon**

½ teaspoon **allspice**

4. Pour combined chocolate mixture over the cubed bread in the baking dish. Stir to saturate all bread. Cover and let rest for one hour at room temperature.

5. Preheat oven to 350 degrees. Cover baking dish with aluminum foil and bake 35-40 minutes, or until the center is firm and a toothpick inserted into it comes out mostly clean. Cut into 9 squares and serve warm.

tips by Tara

Add a tablespoon or 2 of dark rum to give the pudding a Caribbean flare. Serve topped with whipped cream, ice cream, or vanilla yogurt. Reheat any leftovers in microwave before serving.

desserts

Prep Time	Cook Time		Serves	2
15 mins	**40** mins		**9**	**Quart**

temp-tations
presentable ovenware
by Tara

Triple Chocolate Brownies

These brownies are an overload of thick, velvety chocolate! With cocoa powder, chocolate syrup, and milk chocolate chips, these are more decadent than boxed mixes and almost as easy to make. For best results, bake in a 2 quart temp-tations® square baking dish and slice 3 rows by 3 rows to make 9 thick brownies.

1. Preheat oven to 350 degrees. Spray a 2 quart temp-tations® baking dish with nonstick cooking spray.

2. In a large mixing bowl, microwave butter for 45-60 seconds, or until melted and hot. Immediately whisk in cocoa powder until completely dissolved.

3. Whisk chocolate syrup, sugar, eggs, and vanilla extract into the cocoa and butter mixture until all are combined.

4. Using a rubber spatula, fold in flour and baking powder until a batter that is free of lumps is created.

Shopping List

nonstick cooking spray

1 stick **butter** or **margarine**

½ cup **cocoa powder**

3 tablespoons **chocolate syrup**

1 cup **sugar**

2 large **eggs**

1 teaspoon **vanilla extract**

1 cup **flour**

¾ teaspoon **baking powder**

½ cup **milk chocolate chips**

5. Fold chocolate chips into the batter and then pour all into the greased baking dish. Bake 35-40 minutes, or until edges begin to crisp up and center is set. Let cool at least 10 minutes before slicing into 9 squares.

tips by Tara

Semi-sweet, white chocolate, or peanut butter chips can be used in place of the milk chocolate chips, though I prefer the milk chocolate, as the cocoa powder is dark enough that when the two are combined, these come out nice and fudgy.

desserts

| shown in temp-tations® Old World 1.5 quart mixing bowl

Prep Time
15
mins

Chill Time
1
hour

Serves
8

1.5
Quart

temp-tations
presentable ovenware
by Tara

Watergate Salad

This "green salad" is made with anything but lettuce! A traditional potluck dish of pistachio pudding, pineapple, marshmallows, and nuts. I prefer mine with a little cottage cheese mixed in when serving at a picnic or barbeque, as it usually ends up on everybody's plate as more of a side dish than dessert. But if I am serving it solely for dessert, I usually skip the cottage cheese and keep everything sweet.

1. Place instant pistachio pudding mix, crushed pineapple with juice, and cottage cheese in a 1.5 quart temp-tations® mixing bowl or circular baking dish, and stir until well combined. (You can use a 2 quart baking dish for easier mixing, but the presentation won't be as full.)

2. Fold miniature marshmallows and pecans into the mixture.

Shopping List

1 box (**3-4 ounce**) **instant pistachio pudding mix**

1 can (**20** ounces) **crushed pineapple**

¾ cup **cottage cheese**, optional

1 rounded cup **miniature marshmallows**

½ cup **chopped pecans**

4 ounces (½ tub) **regular** or **light non-dairy whipped topping**

3. Fold the non-dairy whipped topping into the mixture, swirling together until almost entirely combined, but leaving a few swirls of white for presentation.

4. Refrigerate for at least 1 hour before serving.

tips by Tara

A small box of sugar free instant pistachio pudding can also be used in place of the regular pudding. You can also make this with 1 smaller can (14-16 ounces) of crushed pineapple and 1 small can of Mandarin oranges (8-10 ounces) to make things a little more interesting. And though it may sound strange at first, adding ½ of a cup of diced celery is also really good!

desserts

Pumpkin Pie Squares with Crunchy Pecan Topping

Not only do these pumpkin pie squares—an old family recipe—have a crunchy pecan topping similar to a pecan pie, but they also have a quick and easy oatmeal crust at the bottom. My family makes them all fall and winter, not just on the holidays!

1. Preheat oven to 350 degrees. Spray a 4 quart temp-tations® baking dish with nonstick cooking spray.

2. In a mixing bowl, combine all crust ingredients and then transfer to the greased baking dish, pressing crust down firmly to set.

3. Combine filling ingredients in the (now empty) mixing bowl and then pour evenly over the crust. Bake 45 minutes or until the filling is springy and almost entirely set.

4. Combine all topping ingredients and sprinkle over the baked squares. Bake an additional 15 minutes, until topping is browned. Cool to room temperature before cutting into 16 squares. Serve topped with whipped cream, if desired.

Shopping List

nonstick cooking spray

CRUST

½ cup **rolled oats**

1 cup **all purpose flour**

½ cup **light brown sugar**

½ cup **butter** or **margarine**, melted

FILLING

1 (**20** ounce) can **pumpkin pie filling**

1 (**12** ounce) can **evaporated milk**

TOPPING

1 cup **chopped pecans**

½ cup **light brown sugar**

2 tablespoons **butter** or **margarine**, melted

tips by Tara

You can substitute 1 (16 ounce) can cooked pumpkin, ¾ cup sugar, 2 teaspoons pumpkin pie spice, and ½ teaspoon salt for the canned pumpkin pie filling.

desserts

Bimbi's Lunch Box Cake

My mother-in-law Barbara, or "Bimbi", makes these delicious cake squares that stay moist for up to an entire week. She doesn't remember where she got the idea to mix fruit cocktail into a cake, but the result makes a perfect take-along cake for lunches, picnics, or even a mid-day snack. Just don't call it fruit cake!

1. Preheat oven to 350 degrees. Spray a 4 quart temp-tations® baking dish (my 13x9 dish works best) with nonstick cooking spray.

2. In a large mixing bowl, combine flour, baking soda, salt, brown sugar, eggs, butter, and juice of the fruit cocktail. Mix extremely well, until smooth and combined.

3. Fold fruit cocktail into the batter and then pour all into the greased baking dish.

4. Top cake with chocolate chips and walnuts, and bake 35-40 minutes, or until golden brown. Let cool 10 minutes before cutting into squares.

Shopping List

nonstick cooking spray

2 rounded cups all purpose flour

2 teaspoons baking soda

1 teaspoon salt

¾ cup light brown sugar

2 large eggs

¼ cup butter or **margarine**, softened

1 can (14-16 ounces) fruit cocktail, undrained

½ cup semi-sweet chocolate chips

½ cup chopped walnuts, optional

tips by Tara

Pecans can be used in place of the walnuts and ½ cup of sweetened coconut can be added to the batter for even more deliciousness!

desserts

| shown transferred to a temp-tations® Old World cake pedestal

Prep Time
10 mins

Cook Time
2 mins

Serves
16

1.5 Quart

temp-tations
presentable ovenware
by Tara

Microwave "Peanut Butter Cup" Fudge

I give a lot of my temp-tations® as gifts, and one of my favorite things to do is actually make a treat like this fudge in one of the dishes in the set before I gift it! Of course, the person receiving the gift doesn't have to know that this fudge only takes 2 minutes in the microwave to make!

1. Liberally spray a 1.5 quart temp-tations® square baking dish with nonstick cooking spray.

2. Add confectioners sugar and cocoa powder to a large temp-tations® mixing bowl and stir until mixed. Sifting the sugar will give you the best results without any small lumps in the finished fudge, but is not entirely necessary.

3. Stir in milk and melted butter, until mostly combined. You may not be able to get all of the sugar off the sides of the bowl, but that is fine.

Shopping List

nonstick cooking spray
1 box (**1** pound) **confectioners sugar**
½ cup **unsweetened cocoa powder**
¼ cup **milk**
¼ cup **butter** or **margarine**, melted
½ cup **shelled peanuts**
¾ cup **peanut butter morsels**

4. Microwave on high for 2 minutes, just until bubbling. Remove from microwave, add the shelled peanuts and immediately stir mixture until smooth and all powdered sugar is dissolved.

5. Quickly pour the hot fudge mixture into the greased 1.5 quart baking dish, shaking from side to side to let it settle. Then immediately sprinkle peanut butter morsels over top, lightly pressing them down into the fudge. Cool on counter for 15 minutes before chilling for 1 hour. Cut into 16 squares to serve.

tips by Tara

The fudge will solidify quickly, so it is best to have the greased dish, peanuts, and peanut butter morsels ready and measured before microwaving in step 4.

desserts

Prep Time
20
mins

Chill Time
2+
hours

Serves
8

2.5
Quart

temp-tations
presentable ovenware
by Tara

Mint and Chocolate Cookie Mousse

This mousse is like a light and fluffy version of mint chocolate chip ice cream—only better—as it uses crushed Oreo style cookies instead of chocolate chips! Serve in parfait glasses or piled high in some of my smaller temp-tations® dishes, such as my 4 ounce muffin cups with tray.

1. In an electric mixer, or using a hand mixer in a large mixing bowl, beat cream and confectioners sugar until peaks are forming and it is nearly whipped cream. Transfer this mixture to a 2.5 quart temp-tations® baking dish.

2. Using the electric mixer once again, beat together pudding mix, peppermint extract, and milk, until the mixture is nice and thick.

Shopping List

1 ¾ cups **heavy whipping cream**

2 tablespoons **confectioners sugar**

2 boxes (**3 ½ ounces each**) **instant vanilla pudding mix**

1 ¼ teaspoons **peppermint extract**

2 cups **milk**

8 **chocolate sandwich cookies** (like Oreos), crushed

3. Gently fold the pudding mixture into the whipped cream mixture in the baking dish, and then fold in crushed chocolate sandwich cookies.

4. Cover and refrigerate for at least 2 hours before serving. Spoon into individual dishes to serve, topping each with 1 whole chocolate sandwich cookie.

tips by Tara

You can add 4-5 drops of green food coloring to the pudding mixture in step 2 to add a nice light green color to the mousse, more reminiscent of mint chocolate chip ice cream.

desserts

Menu Planners

One of the biggest requests that I received when I first told others that I was working on a book was to include a section like this one, which details how to put together an entire meal of dishes that wonderfully complement each other *in* dishes that were designed to complement each other. Though I am sure you will come up with a few combinations of your own, I hope you enjoy my suggestions!

Tara

Prep Time
45
mins

Cook Time
1.5
hours

Serves
8

temp-tations
presentable ovenware
by Tara

Pizza Party

I still have very fond memories of school, and those days that our class would be rewarded with a pizza party. Of course, they never gave us Raspberry Cheesecake Bars in school, but they sure should have!

This menu starts off with my Greek Pasta Salad, though not specifically Italian, this Mediterranean appetizer shares much of the same flavors of Italian food. A few hours before your party, prepare the pasta on the stove at the same time that you are baking the Raspberry Cheesecake Bars. Chill both and all you'll have to do is take them out of the fridge to serve.

The Deep Dish Pepperoni Pizza is prepped in only minutes and once that's in the oven, it's time to have some fun! These days, my favorite thing about a pizza party is that there is no homework!

APPETIZER

Greek Pasta Salad page **19**

MAIN COURSE

Deep Dish Pepperoni Pizza page **95**

DESSERT

Raspberry Cheesecake Bars page **179**

OTHER CHOICES

Making the pizza atop my recipe for Focaccia Bread, recipe page: 23, will make your event a little bit more homemade and authentic. Serve my Baked Three Cheese Spaghetti, recipe page: 129, in place of the Greek Pasta Salad to fully concrete an Italian themed evening.

Prep Time

25
mins

Cook Time

1.75
hours

Serves

6-8

temp-tations
presentable ovenware
by Tara

Family Fun Night

Bring out your favorite board game and gather the whole family around for a meal and games. Real quality family time should not be a thing of the past! With four very kid friendly dishes, this menu may have kids begging to set the table!

The quickest way to prepare all four of these dishes is to start by making the Traditional Baked Macaroni and Cheese, and prep the Corn Dog Casserole as it's baking. Once the mac and cheese is done, cover it with aluminum foil and set aside. Lower the oven to 375 and bake the Corn Dog Casserole. While that is baking, make the fudge in the microwave (It will be fully set in time for dessert.) In the last 10 minutes of the casserole baking, place the covered Mac and Cheese into the oven alongside casserole, and then make the Green Beans Almondine in the microwave.

MAIN COURSE

Corn Dog Casserole page **107**

SIDE

Traditional Baked Macaroni and Cheese page **127**

SIDE

Green Beans Almondine page **151**

DESSERT

Microwave "Peanut Butter Cup" Fudge page **193**

OTHER CHOICES

My Family Favorite Meatloaf, recipe page: 111, is a good choice in place of the Corn Dog Casserole.

Prep Time
35 mins

Cook Time
65 mins

Serves
2+

temp-tations
presentable ovenware
by Tara

Picnic Lunch

My temp-tations® thermal tote makes picnics a breeze. But even if you are just camping out in your own backyard, you are sure to enjoy this menu of lunchtime favorites.

Preparing the Orange and Cream Gelatin Parfait the night before will ensure that it is well set in the morning. Then, simply prepare the Spinach Pie and prep the Toasted Tuscan Turkey Subs as the pie is baking. As soon as the pie is done, place it in my thermal tote bag. Raise the oven temperature to 425 and bake the subs. When they are done, add them to the tote bag (placing the pie on top). You're ready to go! Just be sure to bring the gelatin parfait along outside of my thermal tote, as you don't want it in there with all that hot food!

MAIN COURSE

Toasted Tuscan Turkey Subs page **89**

SIDE DISH

Spinach Pie page **161**

DESSERT

Orange and Cream Gelatin Parfait page **177**

OTHER CHOICES

My Tuna Melt Bagels, recipe page: 63, are a good choice in place of the toasted subs and my Watergate Salad, recipe page: 189, is definitely a picnic dessert staple (though some would argue that it is a side dish)!

Prep Time
25
mins

Cook Time
4
hours

Serves
8

temp-tations
presentable ovenware
by Tara

Holiday Dinner

This book is loaded with recipes suitable for a hearty holiday dinner. With an Orange and Honey Glazed Ham, Apricot Glazed Carrots, and Green Beans with Cherries and Candied Pecans, this holiday menu includes a bounty of different fruits.

For the easiest preparation, make the pound cake the night before, wrapping in plastic wrap after cooling. Both vegetables are microwavable, so they are easily prepped and cooked as the ham bakes. Simply microwave each vegetable 1-2 minutes more right before serving to ensure that they both arrive to the table hot.

MAIN COURSE

Holiday Honey Ham page 103

SIDE

Green Beans with Cherries and Candied Pecans page 145

SIDE

Apricot Glazed Carrots page 157

DESSERT

Chocolate Chip Pound Cake page 181

OTHER CHOICES

Try making my Herb Roasted Turkey Breast, recipe page: 79, in place of the ham. My Cranberry Sweet Potato Casserole, recipe page: 154, is an obviously good choice in place of the carrots. Pecan Pie, recipe page: 173, bakes up a little bit quicker for dessert.

Tara McConnell grew up in a small town one hour outside of New York City with her parents and sister. She is a graduate of West Virginia Wesleyan College and has been working for CSA, Inc., a marketing company specializing in electronic retailing, ever since. In 2004, with their input and support, Tara was able to develop and bring her concept for temp-tations® presentable ovenware to reality.

ACKNOWLEDGEMENTS

A special thank you to my entire family and all of my friends for their love and devotion.

To Ed Tesher, Eric Levine, and Steve Giambruno for all of their support, without that this book would not be possible.

Thanks to temp-tations® and all of my loyal fans my life has been forever changed. I am overwhelmed each and every time you welcome me into your home.

Tara

RECIPE INDEX

Get the latest "dish" straight from Tara and share
your experiences with temp-tations® presentable ovenware at

www.temp-tations.com

temp-tations®
presentable ovenware
by Tara